The Lady & Sons Savannah Country Cookbook

ALSO BY PAULA DEEN

Paula Deen Cuts the Fat

Paula Deen's Southern Cooking Bible

Paula Deen's The Deen Family Cookbook

Paula Deen's Kitchen Wisdom and Recipe Journal

Christmas with Paula Deen

Paula Deen: It Ain't All About the Cookin'

Paula Deen Celebrates!

Paula Deen & Friends: Living It Up, Southern Style

The Lady & Sons Just Desserts

*The Lady & Sons, Too!: A Whole New Batch
of Recipes from Savannah*

Paula Deen's Cookbook for the Lunch-Box Set

Paula Deen's My First Cookbook

Paula Deen's Savannah Style

PAULA DEEN

The Lady & Sons Savannah Country Cookbook

INTRODUCTION BY
JOHN BERENDT

PDV

Paula Deen Ventures
2391 Downing Ave.
Thunderbolt, GA 31404

This work was privately published in different form in 1997
under the title *Favorite Recipes of the Lady & Her Friends*.

Library of Congress Cataloging-in-Publication Data
Deen, Paula.
The Lady & Sons Savannah country cookbook / Paula Deen;
introduction by John Berendt.
p.   cm.
Previously published under title:
Favorite Recipes of the Lady & Her Friends.
Includes index.
ISBN 978-1-943016-00-6
1. Cookery, American—Southern style. 2. Cookery—Georgia—
Savannah. 3. Lady & Sons (Restaurant) I. Deen, Paula.
Favorite Recipes of the Lady & Her Friends. II. Title.
TX715.2.S68D44 1998
641.5975—dc21 97-41561

Manufactured in the United States of America

20 19 18 17 16 15   10 9 8 7 6 5 4 3 2 1

Book design by Victoria Wong

*The most devoted supporters and confidants
of my adult life have been my Aunt Peggy
and Uncle George Ort. It is to Aunt Peggy
and in fond memory of my Uncle George
that this book is most affectionately dedicated.*

A Note from The Lady

Growing up in Albany, Georgia, I used to spend hours at a time in my Grandmother Paul's kitchen at River Bend. Grandmother Paul was a wonderful cook, and she handed down her love of cooking to her three daughters. They in turn passed this love on to me. My life has been surrounded by the many wonderful cooks in my family, and I have been blessed by them through their stories and their food.

In 1989, newly divorced and unemployed, I was living in Savannah and was determined to succeed. Using the cooking skills I learned as a child, I invested my last two hundred dollars in a catering business that I started with my two sons, Jamie and Bobby. I had decided to follow in my grandmother's footsteps.

After a few years of local catering, high demand helped my small-scale business evolve into The Lady & Sons Restaurant. My sons and I function as owners, proprietors, chefs, and hosts. We and our staff are dedicated to providing the finest home-cooked meals in an atmosphere of true Southern hospitality.

I hope my story will inspire others to accept the challenges that life offers. My experience proves that whenever one door closes, another one always opens. I hope you will enjoy these favorite recipes of mine. They have been created with love, sweat, and tears.

There are many people in our lives who deserve a great big thank you for helping us produce this book. They include our outstanding staff, the many wonderful customers who have passed through our restaurant doors, the small businesses in the area who have helped support us, and, of course, our dear family and friends.

Paula

...And a Tribute from Her Sons

Our mother, Paula Deen, is a true symbol of strength and perseverance. This book is a product of her twenty-hour workdays. It is her "third child," and she has nourished and cherished this book just as she has cared for her two sons, in a way that only a mother could do. This book spans many years and many jobs; from homemaker to bank teller to caterer to restaurant owner, our mom's dreams for the future have come true.

Thanks to our mother, these are now the best days of our lives. We have more pride in this lady than can possibly be imagined. She has our undying adoration and our commitment to follow in her direction. Mother is a remarkable lady. We hope you enjoy her wonderful cookbook.

We love you, Mom.

Jamie and Bobby

*If you are lucky enough to be in
the Savannah area, we would love
for you to stop by the restaurant.
Please visit us at:*

**The Lady & Sons
102 West Congress Street
Savannah, GA 31401
(912) 233-2600**

*If you can't get to Savannah to sample
the wonderful food at The Lady & Sons,
you can still taste the dishes at home.
The recipes in this book that we serve
at our restaurant are followed by:*

❦ ❦ ❦ The Lady & Sons

Contents

Desserts / 131

Cooking Tips from The Lady / 179
Index / 181
Acknowledgments / 193

John Berendt

Midnight in the Garden of Good and Evil

Friends planning a trip to Savannah usually ask me for travel tips, and I'm always happy to oblige. Naturally, I suggest a walk through the city's twenty-two sumptuous garden squares and a visit to a few of the museum houses. I tell them not to leave Savannah without taking a short excursion to Bonaventure Cemetery, surely one of the most peaceful sanctuaries on earth, with its avenues of live oaks hung with Spanish moss and its romantic statuary set among flowering shrubs and gentle breezes from the meandering inland waterway.

Then I tell them about food.

I tick off a few of my favorite Savannah eating establishments: Williams Seafood, where locals line up for shrimp, oysters, and crabs that are hauled off fishing boats at a dock a mere stone's throw from the table; Johnny Harris, a tradition for special family occasions since the twenties and known for its barbecued lamb sandwiches; Mrs. Wilkes's, one of America's true culinary landmarks, which lists itself in the phone book simply as "Wilkes L H Mrs, 107 W Jones St," and where lunch is still served at big tables for ten in the old boardinghouse style.

I also tell Savannah-bound friends that if they want a short course in the meaning of Southern cooking—the flavors, the ambience, indeed the very *heart* of Southern cooking—they should drop in at the Lady & Sons. The Lady is a hugely popular downtown eatery that serves the whole gamut of Southern dishes and starts serving you steaming, fresh-out-of-the-oven cheese biscuits while you're waiting on line for a table and then keeps a steady flow coming to you all during your meal.

Paula Deen is the gentle force behind the restaurant and the cookbook you now hold in your hands. Lucky you.

Southern cooking is a hand-me-down art, and that's how Paula Deen came into it. Her grandfather drove a dry-cleaning truck, but he knew all along he had a jewel in Paula's grandmother, because she was a fantastic cook. So he bought her a hot-dog stand in Hapeville, Georgia, in the early forties, and put her to work, with Paula's mother waiting on tables. They did so well they moved up to country steak and creamed potatoes. "The reason I can remember they served steak," says Paula, "is because one day a customer got fresh with my mother, and she slapped him with a piece of steak."

Paula spent whole days in the kitchen with her grandmother, learning the techniques as well as the intention of Southern food. "You have to understand," she says, "Southern cooking comes from within. We show our love for someone through the kitchen, through food. We bake a pie or a cake as a welcoming gift or as a show of support in tough times. Southern cooking is comfort food. It's flavorful and filling, and it makes you feel good."

Authentic Southern food is not about pretension. "It does not require a sophisticated palate," says Paula. "It's poor-man's food. Kids don't have to acquire a taste for it. They love it from the start."

And Southern food is distinctly Southern. "Nothing's flown in," she says. "It's all home-grown. There's no quail, no pheasant, no filet mignon, no foie gras, no truffles, no snails, no caviar, and no crêpes. Southern dishes do not require split-second timing. They do not 'fall' in the oven. We don't go in for ornate presentation, either, or sculpted desserts. We just heap food on the plate."

Paula knows that some aspects of Southern cooking are disdained by outsiders. "There are some things we do that would make a French chef sick," she says. "Like, for instance, the way we make red-eye gravy—country ham cooked in a skillet with water and strong coffee. But let the French chef taste it, and he'll get over being sick real quick!"

Southern cooks are proud of their cuisine, and they are not hesitant to tell you that, stacked up against any other cookery, it comes out on top. As Paula says, with a wink to me, "I've never heard anybody say,

'Gee, golly, I can't wait to get up to New York so I can have some of that good Yankee food.' "

The staples of classic Southern food, as laid out in this book, are butter, sugar, salt, pepper, hot sauce, vinegar, ham hocks, and, to lay it on the line: fat. "We can make concessions for the health-conscious," says Paula, "by doing things like using smoked turkey wings instead of ham hocks. But a better approach for weight watchers is to look at Southern food as a treat and just go with it."

Southern food is tied in with the Southern experience, which is a heady combination of good times and bad. Paula has had her share of both. She lived the life of a Southern princess for her first nineteen years—happy, pampered, and carefree. Then her father dropped dead, and four years later her mother died of a broken heart and bone cancer. Paula had to go to work. She was head teller at a bank for a while until a bank robber put a gun to her head and she decided she wasn't cut out for banking.

With her marriage coming to an end and creditors closing in some years ago, Paula got into what she knew best: cooking. She took two hundred dollars and opened a service with her two sons and their girlfriends, wheeling hot lunches through office buildings in downtown Savannah. They called it the Bag Lady. Paula got up every morning at five o'clock and made 250 meals in her own kitchen—grilled chicken, lasagna, trio sandwiches, and custards, banana pudding, and fruit salad for dessert. "If the business hadn't made it, I was looking the Salvation Army square in the face," she says. But it did make it, and Paula's customers insisted she open a restaurant, which she did.

"The day we opened," she recalls, "I was overdrawn at two banks, not just one. I didn't even have enough money for the parking meter. My banker called, and I said to him, 'Just let me open my doors.' He did, and the people came flooding in."

And they still do. Businessmen, housewives, lawyers, students, tourists, and celebrities. The mayor is a regular customer. Paula has had to extend her hours to accommodate all the business.

Ms. Deen is an irresistible example of that extraordinary phenomenon of Southern womanhood, the steel magnolia. She is always appealing and gracious but possessed of an unfailing survival instinct—a necessary character trait for a Southern cook to make it.

And make it, she has. If you go to Savannah, you can understand the reason for it by sampling her famous cheese biscuits, her hoe cakes, her sensational gooey butter cakes, and all the rest. However, if you can't wait till then, you don't have to. Just follow the Lady's instructions on the following pages and you'll know soon enough what all the fuss is about.

JOHN BERENDT
New York
January 1998

Appetizers

COLD APPETIZERS

Pecan-Stuffed Dates

YIELDS APPROXIMATELY 30

One 8-ounce box pitted dates   *10 to 12 slices bacon*
30 pecan halves

Preheat oven to 400 degrees. Stuff each date with a pecan half. Cut each slice of bacon into 3 pieces. Wrap 1 piece around each stuffed date and secure with a toothpick. Bake until bacon is crisp, 12 to 15 minutes. Drain and serve.

Georgia Sugared Peanuts

YIELDS 2 CUPS

1 cup sugar   *2 cups raw shelled peanuts, skins on*
½ cup water   *¼ teaspoon salt*

Preheat oven to 300 degrees. Dissolve sugar and salt in water in saucepan over medium heat. Add peanuts. Continue to cook, stirring frequently, until peanuts are completely sugared (coated and no syrup left). Pour onto ungreased cookie sheet, spreading so that peanuts are separated as much as possible. Bake for approximately 30 minutes, stirring at 5-minute intervals. Let cool and serve.

Hot Asparagus Dip

YIELDS 3 TO 4 CUPS

Two 12-ounce cans asparagus
  spears
1½ cups mayonnaise
1½ cups freshly grated Parmesan
  cheese, plus additional for
  sprinkling

2 cloves garlic, chopped
Salt and pepper to taste

Preheat oven to 350 degrees. Drain and chop asparagus. Add to remaining ingredients and mix; pour into baking dish. Bake for 20 to 25 minutes until slightly brown and bubbly. Remove from oven and sprinkle with additional Parmesan cheese. Serve hot with lightly toasted French bread rounds.

Hot Crab Canapé

SERVES 6 TO 8

One 8-ounce package cream
  cheese, softened
1 tablespoon milk
⅓ cup mayonnaise
1½ teaspoons horseradish

8 ounces crabmeat, picked free
  of shell
2 tablespoons chopped onion
¼ teaspoon garlic salt

Preheat oven to 350 degrees. With an electric mixer, mix all ingredients in a bowl. Place mixture in a shallow ovenproof casserole dish. Bake for 15 to 20 minutes or microwave until warm (2 to 3 minutes). Serve with crackers. This may be frozen for future use.

Mini Onion Quiches

YIELDS 2 DOZEN

¾ cup crushed saltine crackers
4 tablespoons (½ stick) butter,
    melted
1 cup chopped green onion with
    tops
2 tablespoons butter

2 eggs
1 cup milk
½ teaspoon salt
¼ teaspoon pepper
1 cup grated Swiss cheese

Preheat oven to 300 degrees. Combine cracker crumbs and melted butter. Divide crumbs among mini muffin tins that have been sprayed with no-stick cooking spray. Sauté onion for 10 minutes in 2 tablespoons butter. Cool, then divide evenly on top of cracker crumbs. Beat eggs; add milk, salt, pepper, and Swiss cheese. Pour by spoonfuls on top of onion in tins. Do not fill to top, as they will run over. Bake until set, about 15 to 20 minutes. Do not overbake. May be stored in refrigerator or freezer. Warm in oven before serving.

Sausage Balls

YIELDS APPROXIMATELY 3 DOZEN

3 cups Bisquick
2 cups grated Cheddar cheese

1 pound fresh ground sausage
    (hot or mild)

Preheat oven to 350 degrees. Mix all ingredients together. If not moist enough, add a little water. Form mixture into 1-inch balls. Bake for 15 minutes. Drain on paper towels. Serve warm. This freezes well before or after baking.

Cheese-Stuffed Mushrooms

YIELDS 2 DOZEN

24 fresh mushrooms, stems removed
One 10-ounce package frozen
  chopped spinach
2 ounces cream cheese
4 ounces feta cheese

½ cup finely chopped green onion
  with tops
Salt to taste
1 cup grated Parmesan cheese

Preheat oven to 350 degrees. Wipe mushroom caps clean with a damp paper towel. Thaw spinach in colander; squeeze out as much moisture as possible. In mixing bowl, combine all ingredients except mushrooms and Parmesan cheese. Mix well. Fill mushroom caps with mixture and place on a cookie sheet. Sprinkle Parmesan cheese on top. Bake for 15 to 20 minutes. Serve warm.

Sesame Chicken Strips

SERVES 8 TO 10

6 skinless boneless chicken breast
  halves
1 cup sour cream
1 tablespoon lemon juice, or juice
  of ½ lemon
2 teaspoons celery salt
2 teaspoons Worcestershire sauce

½ teaspoon salt
¼ teaspoon pepper
2 cloves garlic, minced
1 cup dry bread crumbs
⅓ cup sesame seeds
4 tablespoons (½ stick) butter,
  melted

Lightly grease a 15 × 10-inch jelly roll pan. Cut chicken crosswise into ½-inch strips. In a large bowl, combine sour cream, lemon juice, celery salt, Worcestershire sauce, salt, pepper, and garlic. Mix well. Add chicken to mixture, coat well, and cover. Refrigerate at least 8 hours or overnight. Preheat oven to 350 degrees. In medium bowl, combine bread crumbs and sesame seeds. Remove chicken strips from sour cream mixture. Roll in crumb mixture, coating evenly. Arrange in single layer in prepared pan. Spoon butter evenly over chicken. Bake for 40 to 45 minutes or until chicken is tender and golden brown. Serve with honey mustard.

Oysters in the Patty Shell

YIELDS 30 PIECES

½ pound mushrooms, chopped
3 tablespoons butter
3 tablespoons all-purpose flour
1 cup milk
½ teaspoon salt
¼ teaspoon celery salt
Pepper to taste

1 teaspoon lemon juice
1 cup shelled fresh oysters, drained
*   and chopped*
Eight 1-ounce prebaked mini-
*   piecrusts or patty shells*
*   (approximately 3 inches in size)*
Fresh parsley, for garnish

Sauté mushrooms in butter until tender. Blend in flour and cook until bubbly. Gradually add milk; cook until smooth and thickened, stirring constantly. Add salt, celery salt, pepper, lemon juice, and oysters. Cook over medium-low heat until oysters start to curl up (about 5 minutes), stirring occasionally. Serve in mini-piecrusts or patty shells. If desired, garnish with parsley.

Brie en Croûte #1

SERVES 8

1 sheet frozen puff pastry (package
*   comes with 2 sheets)*
1 tablespoon butter
½ cup chopped walnuts

⅛ teaspoon ground cinnamon
1 small wheel of Brie (8 ounces)
¼ cup brown sugar
1 egg, beaten

Preheat oven to 375 degrees. Defrost one sheet of puff pastry for approximately 15 to 20 minutes and unfold (place remaining sheet in freezer for later use). Melt butter in a saucepan over medium heat. Sauté walnuts in butter until golden brown, approximately 5 minutes. Stir in cinnamon, coating nuts well. Place mixture on top of wheel of Brie. Sprinkle brown sugar over the mixture. Carefully place pastry sheet over wheel of Brie (make sure Brie is centered). Gently pick Brie up with pastry hanging over edge and fold the pastry under Brie. Trim excess pastry with scissors so Brie lies flat, and seal all edges to prevent leakage. To give an extra-special look to the Brie, I like to cut the left-over pastry into heart shapes, flowers, etc., and place them onto the pastry on top of the Brie. Brush beaten egg over top and sides of Brie, then place cutouts on top (the egg will secure them); brush cutouts with egg. Place wrapped Brie on an ungreased cookie sheet and bake for 20 minutes until pastry is golden brown. Serve with top-quality crackers.

Brie en Croûte #2

SERVES 8

1 sheet frozen puff pastry (package comes with 2 sheets)
1 tablespoon butter
¼ cup chopped pecans or walnuts

1 small wheel of Brie (8 ounces)
½ cup raspberry jam
2 eggs, beaten

Preheat oven to 375 degrees. Defrost one sheet of puff pastry for approximately 15 to 20 minutes and unfold (place remaining sheet in freezer for later use). Melt butter in a saucepan over medium heat. Sauté nuts in butter until golden brown, approximately 5 minutes. Place nuts on top of Brie and spread jam on top of nuts. Gently roll pastry with a rolling pin to increase the size of the sheet 1 to 2 inches in each direction. Brush both sides of the sheet with beaten egg. Center the wheel of Brie on top of the pastry sheet. Bring all four corners of the sheet together above Brie and twist slightly to form a "bundle." Tie gathered pastry with kitchen/cooking string (tie string in the form of a bow). Work with pastry until you are satisfied with the "bundle" shape. Place "bundle" on an ungreased cookie sheet and bake for 20 to 25 minutes until pastry is golden brown. Serve with top-quality crackers.

Naked Buffalo Wings

SERVES 2

½ pound (2 sticks) butter
½ cup The Lady & Sons Signature
    Hot Sauce
Salt and black pepper to taste

1 pound chicken wings, each wing
    cut at joint to yield wingette
    and drumette
Peanut oil for frying
    (or vegetable or canola oil)

In a small saucepan over low heat, heat butter and hot sauce just until butter melts; keep warm on stove top. Salt and pepper the chicken. In a deep fryer or Dutch oven, heat oil to 375 degrees. Deep-fry chicken, 8 to 10 pieces at a time, for 10 to 12 minutes, turning once or twice. Drain chicken on a wire cooling rack for 30 seconds. Transfer warm buffalo sauce to a very large mixing bowl. In batches, toss fried chicken in buffalo sauce and remove with a slotted spoon.

NOTE: Adjust ratio of hot sauce to butter for a milder or hotter sauce.

Bacon Wraps

YIELDS 2 DOZEN

1 cup grated Parmesan cheese
2 teaspoons garlic salt or powder
12 slices bacon

Twenty-four 4½-inch-long sesame
    breadsticks (one package)

Preheat oven to 350 degrees. Mix Parmesan cheese with garlic salt or powder in a shallow bowl and set aside. Cut the slices of bacon in half so that each is approximately 5 inches long. Wrap one piece of bacon around a breadstick, starting at one end of breadstick and finishing at other end (I find that bacon adheres to sesame breadsticks better than plain breadsticks). Place on a cookie sheet lined with parchment paper. Repeat this process, using all of breadsticks. Bake for approximately 15 minutes, or until bacon is browned. Remove from cookie sheet and immediately roll bacon wraps in cheese mixture. Let cool and serve at room temperature.

Artichoke and Spinach Dip

YIELDS 3 CUPS

One half of a 10-ounce package
   frozen chopped spinach, thawed
Two 13¾-ounce cans artichoke
   hearts, drained and mashed

½ cup mayonnaise
½ cup sour cream
1½ cups grated Parmesan cheese
Salt and pepper to taste

Preheat oven to 350 degrees. Drain all water from spinach. Mix all ingredients and bake in greased casserole for 30 to 40 minutes. Serve with butter crackers or bagel chips.   ❦ ❦ ❦ **The Lady & Sons**

Barbecue Meatball Appetizer

YIELDS APPROXIMATELY 80 MEATBALLS

1 large onion, finely chopped
2 stalks celery, finely chopped
2 cloves garlic, minced
2 tablespoons olive oil
2 pounds ground beef
1 pound ground pork
1 cup evaporated milk

1 cup dry bread crumbs
2 large eggs
1½ teaspoons salt
2 teaspoons chili powder
½ teaspoon black pepper
12 ounces The Lady's Barbecue
   Sauce (see page 124)

In a small skillet, sauté onion, celery, and garlic in olive oil until onion is translucent. Set aside. In a large mixing bowl, combine beef, pork, evaporated milk, bread crumbs, eggs, onion mixture, salt, chili powder, and pepper. Mix well. Form into 1-inch balls. Arrange in a single layer on cookie sheets lined with waxed paper. Freeze until solid; store in freezer bags until ready to cook. To cook, preheat oven to 350 degrees. Place frozen meatballs in a 9 × 13-inch baking dish; pour barbecue sauce over meatballs. Bake for about 1 hour. Serve warm.

Shrimp Butter

YIELDS APPROXIMATELY 4 CUPS

½ pound (2 sticks) butter, at room
   temperature
1 tablespoon sherry
½ teaspoon lemon zest
1 teaspoon House Seasoning
   (see page 180)
Juice of ½ lemon

Cayenne pepper to taste
Two 3-ounce packages cream cheese,
   softened
2 tablespoons chopped onion
1 pound shrimp, shelled, deveined,
   and cooked

Add all ingredients except shrimp to a food processor. Process until well mixed. Drop in shrimp and process until either pureed or chopped to desired consistency. (This recipe can be pureed to the consistency of butter or left with chunky pieces of shrimp.) Serve on crackers as an appetizer. It is also wonderful served on top of hot grits. (If served with grits, sprinkle grated Cheddar cheese over grits and shrimp butter.)

Italian Roasted Red Peppers

SERVES 8

4 large red bell peppers
1 cup olive oil
2 to 3 cloves garlic, minced
1 tablespoon dried basil,
   or ½ bunch fresh snipped,
   cleaned basil

2 teaspoons salt, or to taste
Pinch of sugar
Ground black pepper to taste

Preheat oven to 450 degrees. Wash red bell peppers and bake until skin is charred; turn periodically to ensure that the skin blackens on all sides. Remove peppers from oven and put into a paper sack. Fold the top of the sack over. Allow peppers to steam in the sack for 30 minutes to 1 hour. Peel the skin from the peppers; pull the peppers into strips, allowing the juice to drip into the bowl where the peppers will go. Toss the peppers with olive oil, minced garlic, basil, salt, sugar, and pepper. Let stand for several hours. Serve peppers on slices of Italian bread or as a side dish.

Southwestern Dip

YIELDS 3 TO 4 CUPS

One 16-ounce can refried beans
One 8-ounce package cream cheese
2 large tomatoes, diced
One half of a 1½-ounce package of
    dried taco seasoning
One 6-ounce carton prepared
    avocado dip

One 4-ounce can chopped ripe olives
1 small onion, chopped
One 4½-ounce can chopped green
    chilies

Layer ingredients in a 9 × 13-inch dish in the order given. Chill for several hours. Serve with tortilla chips.

NOTE: In place of the prepared mix, you may substitute 2 medium ripe avocados, mashed and mixed with 2 tablespoons lemon juice, ½ teaspoon salt, and ¼ teaspoon black pepper.

Pickled Okra Sandwiches

YIELDS 20 TO 24 WHOLE SANDWICHES

One 24-ounce loaf sliced white
    bread
One 8-ounce package cream
    cheese, softened

One 16-ounce jar pickled okra
1 cup finely chopped fresh parsley

Remove crusts from bread. With a rolling pin, roll slices very thin. Coat each slice with cream cheese and place an okra spear in center; roll up. Spread a light coat of cream cheese on each rolled-up sandwich (I like to use my fingers to spread the cream cheese). Roll sandwich in finely chopped parsley. Cut in half, if desired.

Herbed Cream Cheese Round

YIELDS 4 CUPS

Two 8-ounce packages cream
   cheese, softened
1 cup chopped fresh parsley
¾ cup grated Parmesan cheese
¼ cup chopped pine nuts
2 cloves garlic, crushed

1 tablespoon dried basil
¼ teaspoon salt
⅛ teaspoon pepper
⅓ cup olive oil
2 tablespoons butter, melted
2 tablespoons boiling water

Shape cream cheese into a 5½-inch circle on serving dish, making a slight well in center of circle; set aside. Combine parsley with rest of ingredients. Mix well. Spoon onto cream cheese round; garnish with fresh basil sprigs if desired. Cover and chill at least 2 hours. Serve with crackers or toasted pita triangles.

Quick Guacamole-Spinach Dip

YIELDS 2 CUPS

1 package dry guacamole dip mix
   (found in produce departments)
One 8-ounce container soft cream
   cheese

One 10-ounce package frozen
   chopped spinach, thawed
1 large tomato, finely chopped

Combine guacamole mix and cream cheese. Squeeze excess liquid from spinach. Add to cheese mixture. Add tomato. Mix well to combine. Serve with tortilla chips.

Garlic Cheese Spread

YIELDS 2 CUPS

One 8-ounce package cream cheese
One 8-ounce jar Cheez Whiz
¾ teaspoon garlic powder, or to
   taste

⅛ teaspoon seasoned salt
⅛ teaspoon pepper

Combine all ingredients and beat with hand mixer for 2 minutes or until smooth. Serve with freshly toasted French bread.

Creamy Roquefort Dip

YIELDS 2 CUPS

This also makes a wonderful dressing for salads.

½ cup crumbled Roquefort cheese
One 3-ounce package cream
   cheese, softened
½ cup mayonnaise

1 tablespoon lemon juice
1 tablespoon wine vinegar
½ cup sour cream

Blend Roquefort and cream cheese until smooth. Mix in remaining ingredients. Beat well. Chill for 2 hours. Serve with vegetable crudité.

Strawberry Cheese Ring

SERVES APPROXIMATELY 20

I've heard this was our governor and later president Jimmy Carter's favorite cheese dish. His First Lady, Rosalynn Carter, has been credited for making this a famous Southern favorite.

16 ounces sharp Cheddar cheese, grated

One 3-ounce package cream cheese, softened

¾ cup mayonnaise

1 small onion, chopped

1 cup chopped pecans or walnuts

½ teaspoon garlic salt or powder

Cayenne pepper to taste

1 cup strawberry preserves

Combine all ingredients except preserves in a food processor or electric mixer. Mix thoroughly and refrigerate for 2 to 3 hours. Scoop mixture onto a platter. Use your hands to mold mixture into a ring formation (I suggest placing a sheet of wax paper between your hands and the mixture to prevent melting and stickiness). Spread strawberry preserves in center of ring and serve with some good, buttery crackers.

Lightning-Fast White Bean Dip

SERVES 4

One 16-ounce can white kidney beans, rinsed and drained

1 clove garlic, minced

1 tablespoon olive oil

Juice of 1 lemon

1 teaspoon The Lady & Sons Signature Hot Sauce

½ teaspoon ground cumin

1 teaspoon salt

Chopped fresh chives, for garnish

In the bowl of a food processor, combine all ingredients except chives and pulse until smooth. Refrigerate until ready to serve. Garnish with chopped chives. Serve with crisp carrot sticks or toasted pita triangles.

Black Bean Salsa

SERVES 12

Two 15-ounce cans black beans,
 rinsed and drained
One 17-ounce package frozen
 whole-kernel corn, thawed
2 large tomatoes, seeded and
 chopped
1 large avocado, peeled and
 chopped (optional)

1 small onion, chopped
⅛ to ¼ cup chopped fresh cilantro
3 to 4 tablespoons lime juice
1 tablespoon red wine vinegar
Salt and pepper to taste

Mix all ingredients thoroughly in a large bowl. Cover and chill overnight. Taste and add salt, pepper, or more lime juice as necessary. Serve with tortilla chips as an appetizer, or with grilled chicken breast as a meal.

Bobby's Pimento Cheese

YIELDS APPROXIMATELY 2½ TO 3 CUPS

This is my son Bobby's own recipe for pimento cheese. It is a definite favorite.

One 3-ounce package cream cheese,
 softened
1 cup grated sharp Cheddar cheese
1 cup grated Monterey Jack cheese
½ cup mayonnaise

½ teaspoon House Seasoning
 (see page 180)
2 to 3 tablespoons mashed pimentos
1 teaspoon grated onion (optional)
Cracked black pepper to taste

With an electric mixer, beat cream cheese until fluffy. Add remaining ingredients and beat until well blended.

Soups and Salads

SOUPS

SALADS

She Crab Soup

This is a traditional favorite down here. We try to use female crabs, but you can use either male or female.

One 2-pound fish head (preferably
  grouper), eyes, gills, and scales
  removed
1 medium onion, peeled
2 ribs celery, including tops
½ teaspoon salt
½ teaspoon white pepper
¾ cup chopped green onion,
  with tops
2 teaspoons minced garlic
4 tablespoons (½ stick) butter

3 tablespoons all-purpose flour
1 cup heavy cream
1 cup milk
1 pound crabmeat, picked free
  of shell
¼ cup sherry
½ teaspoon lemon-pepper seasoning
1 cup freshly grated Parmesan
  cheese
½ cup chopped fresh chives

To make fish stock, combine fish head, whole onion, celery, salt, and white pepper in a large pot. Cover with 4½ cups of water. Bring pot to a boil, reduce heat, cover pot, and cook for 30 minutes. Remove fish from pot and allow to cool. Separate fish into pieces that resemble picked crabmeat and set aside. Discard celery and onion from stock. Sauté chopped green onion and garlic in butter until tender. Stir in flour, stirring until well blended. Slowly add 2 cups of the fish stock, continuing to cook until smooth and bubbly. Slowly add cream and milk. Stir in fish and crabmeat. Add sherry and lemon-pepper seasoning. Simmer until piping hot; adjust seasoning (sherry, garlic, salt, and pepper) to taste. Serve in bowls topped with cheese and chives.

🦀 🦀 🦀 *The Lady & Sons*

NOTE: You may freeze leftover fish stock for future use. If you wish, you may skip preparing the fish stock and substitute 2 cups chicken stock.

Roasted Red Pepper Soup

SERVES 3 TO 4

1 medium onion, chopped
2 tablespoons butter
4 cloves garlic, minced
2 large red bell peppers, roasted
*   and chopped*

2 tablespoons chopped fresh thyme
Salt and pepper to taste
½ cup white wine
2 cups chicken stock
1 cup heavy cream

Over medium heat, sauté onion in butter until soft. Add garlic, red pepper, thyme, salt, and pepper. Add wine and scald. Lower heat and add chicken stock and cream. Cook 3 to 5 minutes and remove from heat. Put in blender and blend until smooth. Return to saucepan and cook for 5 minutes over medium heat. Serve immediately.

Pot Roast Soup

SERVES 6

1 tablespoon vegetable oil
1 tablespoon butter
1 medium onion, chopped
2 celery stalks, chopped
2 medium carrots, chopped
½ pound cremini mushrooms,
*   quartered*
3 large cloves garlic, chopped
1 tablespoon chopped fresh thyme
2 tablespoons sherry

4 cups low-sodium beef broth
*   (canned or homemade)*
2 tablespoons tomato paste
1½ cups leftover pot roast,
*   shredded into large chunks,*
*   plus leftover gravy*
1 dash of Worcestershire sauce
Kosher salt and freshly ground
*   black pepper to taste*
Fresh parsley, chopped, for garnish

In a large soup pot, heat oil and butter over moderate heat. Add onion, celery, carrots, mushrooms, and garlic and sauté until tender and lightly browned, about 5 minutes. Add thyme and cook, stirring, for 1 minute. Add sherry and stir up any bits that have stuck to the bottom of the pan. Stir in beef broth, tomato paste, and meat with leftover gravy. Simmer, stirring occasionally, about 25 minutes. Taste for seasoning and add Worcestershire sauce, salt, and pepper. Serve in a warmed soup bowl sprinkled with chopped parsley.

Oyster Stew

SERVES 4 TO 5

2 green onions, chopped
2 tablespoons butter
12 ounces fresh raw oysters,
    undrained
1 quart half-and-half or whole
    milk

¼ teaspoon salt
¼ teaspoon white pepper
⅛ teaspoon cayenne pepper

Sauté onion in butter until tender. Add remaining ingredients. Cook over low heat until edges of oysters begin to curl and mixture is hot but not boiling. Serve stew with crackers.

White Bean Chili

SERVES 10 TO 15

1 pound dried navy beans
6 cups chicken stock
4 tablespoons (½ stick) butter
1 tablespoon minced garlic
¾ cup diced onion
1½ green chilies (fresh or canned),
    chopped
1 pound skinless boneless chicken
    breast, finely chopped

1½ tablespoons ground cumin
1 tablespoon dried oregano
1 to 2 teaspoons ground black
    pepper
¾ teaspoon white pepper
½ bunch cilantro, chopped

Wash beans, cover with water, and soak for 2 hours. Drain. Place beans in large pot with chicken stock. Bring to a boil. In saucepan, heat butter and sauté garlic, onion, and chilies for 5 minutes. Add to bean pot. Add chicken, cumin, oregano, black pepper, white pepper, and cilantro. Lower heat to medium and cook, stirring occasionally, for approximately 1½ hours. Serve with corn bread.

Shrimp Bisque

SERVES 6 TO 8

One 10 ¾-ounce can condensed
    cream of mushroom soup
One 10 ¾-ounce can condensed
    cream of chicken soup
Two 12-ounce cans evaporated
    milk

2 tablespoons butter
½ pound cooked shrimp, peeled,
    deveined, and chopped
Dash of Worcestershire sauce
Dash of Tabasco
¼ cup sherry, or to taste

In top of double boiler, heat soups, milk, and butter over boiling water. Add shrimp, Worcestershire sauce, and Tabasco. Stir in sherry to taste. Continue heating until desired temperature. Great served plain or over steamed rice.

Sherried Avocado Bouillon

SERVES 6

Two 10 ¾-ounce cans condensed
    beef broth
1⅓ cups water
¼ cup sherry

2 tablespoons chopped fresh parsley
Salt and pepper to taste
1 medium avocado, peeled and
    finely diced

Heat broth and water to boiling. Add sherry and parsley and season to taste with salt and pepper. Remove from heat and stir in avocado. Pour at once into heated bouillon cups. Garnish with avocado slices, if desired.

The Lady's Chicken Noodle Soup

SERVES 8 TO 10

One 2½- to 3-pound fryer, cut up
3½ quarts water
1 onion, peeled
1½ to 2 teaspoons Italian
   seasoning

1 teaspoon lemon-pepper seasoning
3 cloves garlic, minced
4 bay leaves
3 chicken bouillon cubes
Salt and pepper to taste

Add all ingredients to a pot. Cook until chicken is tender, about 35 to 45 minutes. Remove chicken from pot and set aside to cool. Remove and discard bay leaves and onion. You should have approximately 3 quarts of stock. When chicken is cool enough to touch, pick bones clean, discarding bones, skin, and cartilage. Set chicken aside. For the next step, you will need:

2 cups sliced carrots
2 cups sliced celery, with leafy green
   tops
2½ cups uncooked egg noodles
3 tablespoons minced fresh parsley

⅓ cup grated Parmesan cheese
   (optional)
¾ cup heavy cream (optional)
⅓ cup cooking sherry
Salt and pepper to taste

Bring stock back to a boil, add carrots, and cook for 3 minutes. Add celery and continue to cook for 5 to 10 minutes. Add egg noodles and cook according to directions on package. When noodles are done, add chicken, parsley, cheese, cream, and sherry. Cook for another 2 minutes. Adjust seasoning if needed by adding salt and pepper. Enjoy along with a nice hot crusty loaf of French bread. If you are watching calories, you may leave out the cheese and cream.

❦ ❦ ❦ *The Lady & Sons*

Creamy Cheddar Soup

SERVES 3 TO 4

1 small onion, chopped
2 large pimentos, chopped
3 tablespoons butter
3 tablespoons all-purpose flour
1½ cups chicken stock

1½ cups half-and-half
¾ cup grated sharp Cheddar cheese
Salt and ground black pepper
   to taste
Dash of cayenne pepper (optional)

In a saucepan, sauté onion and pimentos in butter for 5 to 7 minutes. Blend in flour. Add stock and half-and-half. Cook until thick. Add cheese and stir until melted. Add salt and black pepper to taste, and cayenne if desired.

Chicken Chili Stew

SERVES 6

1 tablespoon canola oil
1 medium onion, chopped
1 yellow bell pepper, chopped
3 cloves garlic, chopped
1 small jalapeño chili pepper,
   seeds removed, chopped
1 tablespoon chili powder
Kosher salt to taste
4 cups chicken broth
1 medium sweet potato, peeled
   and cubed

2 cups prepared salsa verde
12 ounces leftover roasted chicken,
   skinned and shredded into
   large pieces
One 15-ounce can pinto beans,
   rinsed and drained
½ cup packed fresh cilantro,
   chopped
Freshly ground black pepper to taste
1 avocado, diced, for garnish
Sour cream, for garnish

In a large pot, heat oil over medium-high heat. Add onion, bell pepper, garlic, and jalapeño chili pepper and sauté until soft, about 4 minutes. Add chili powder and season with salt. Stir in chicken broth, sweet potato, and salsa verde and bring to a boil. Reduce heat and simmer, stirring occasionally, until sweet potato is just tender, about 10 to 12 minutes. Stir in shredded chicken and beans. Reduce heat to moderately low and simmer, covered, for 10 minutes. Stir in cilantro and season with black pepper at end of cooking. Ladle into soup bowls and garnish with diced avocado and dollop of sour cream.

NOTE: You can find salsa verde in the Latin foods section of your grocery store.

Sausage and Lentil Soup

SERVES 8 TO 10

2 tablespoons olive oil
1 pound sausage (chorizo, Polish, etc.)
7 ounces smoked ham, shredded
2 large onions, chopped
1 large green bell pepper, chopped
1 medium carrot, diced
2 cloves garlic, minced
½ teaspoon ground cumin

¾ teaspoon dried thyme
1 bay leaf
8 to 9 cups chicken stock
One 16-ounce can peeled tomatoes, crushed
½ pound dried lentils (1¼ cups)
12 large spinach leaves, cut into small pieces
Salt and pepper to taste

Heat olive oil in a large saucepan over medium heat. Add sausage and cook until done. Remove sausage and place on a platter, allowing time to cool. When cool, slice sausage into ⅛-inch slices. Discard all but 2 tablespoons of drippings from pan. Reheat drippings and add ham, onion, green pepper, and carrot to the saucepan. Cover and cook over medium heat for 15 minutes. Stir in garlic, cumin, thyme, and bay leaf. Cover and cook for 5 more minutes. Add chicken stock, sliced sausage, tomatoes, and lentils. Cover and cook over low heat for 2 hours. As soup cooks, skim off fat that rises to the top. After 2 hours turn off heat and discard bay leaf. Add spinach, salt, and pepper and let stand for 2 to 3 minutes before serving.

Shrimp or Lobster Bisque

SERVES 4 TO 5

8 ounces cooked shrimp or lobster
  meat
2 tablespoons sherry, plus
  additional to taste
Pinch of thyme
3 to 4 green onions with tops,
  chopped
2 tablespoons butter

One 10¾-ounce can condensed
  tomato soup
1 soup can measure of milk
One 10¾-ounce can condensed
  cream of mushroom soup
1 soup can measure of heavy cream
Chopped fresh parsley, for garnish

Finely chop the shrimp or lobster meat and marinate 30 minutes in 2 tablespoons of sherry and the thyme. Sauté onions in butter until soft. Add shrimp or lobster meat and cook over a low heat for 3 to 5 minutes. In a separate bowl, combine tomato soup with milk and blend mushroom soup with cream. Combine the two soup mixtures with the shrimp-lobster sauté. Simmer over low heat for 3 to 5 minutes. Add more sherry to taste. Cool, then mix in blender until thick and smooth. To serve, reheat in a double boiler. Add more sherry to taste and garnish with chopped parsley.

Cream of Artichoke Soup

SERVES 6

Two 13¾-ounce cans artichoke
  hearts, chopped
1½ cups chicken stock
1 cup chopped onion
4 tablespoons (½ stick) butter

One 10¾ ounce can condensed
  cream of mushroom soup
⅓ cup heavy cream
Salt and pepper to taste

Bring artichokes and chicken stock to a boil. In a saucepan, sauté onion in butter and add to mixture. Gradually add mushroom soup to desired thickness. Slowly add cream, stirring constantly. Remove from heat. Add salt and pepper.   🍀 🍀 🍀 **The Lady & Sons**

Simple Southern Ham and Bean Soup

SERVES 6 TO 8

1 tablespoon olive oil
1 tablespoon butter, plus more for
*   garnish*
1 small onion, finely chopped
2 cloves garlic, finely chopped
1½ cups diced leftover ham
2 teaspoons fresh thyme
Two 15-ounce cans white beans,
*   rinsed and drained*

4 cups low-sodium chicken broth
*   (canned or homemade)*
1 bay leaf
4 cups fresh collard greens, cut into
*   thin ribbons (or one 10-ounce*
*   package frozen collard greens)*
Kosher salt and freshly ground
*   black pepper to taste*

Heat oil and butter in a heavy-bottomed pot over medium heat; add onion, garlic, ham, and thyme and cook, stirring occasionally, until onion is soft, about 4 minutes. Add beans, chicken broth, bay leaf, collards, salt, and pepper and simmer, stirring occasionally, for 20 minutes, so flavors can develop. Remove bay leaf before serving. Serve in soup bowls and garnish with a tablespoon of butter on top.

Tomato Dill Soup

SERVES 6

3 cups peeled and diced fresh
*   tomatoes (or one 28-ounce can)*
1 medium onion, chopped
2 cups chicken stock
1 teaspoon chopped garlic
⅓ to ½ cup white wine
1 teaspoon lemon-pepper seasoning

3 tablespoons chopped fresh dill
¾ cup heavy cream
¼ cup chopped fresh parsley
¼ cup grated Parmesan cheese
Salt and coarsely ground black
*   pepper to taste*

In a large pot, mix all ingredients together except heavy cream, parsley, Parmesan, and salt and pepper. Cook over medium heat about 30 minutes, until tomatoes are tender. Add cream, parsley, and Parmesan cheese last. Season with salt and pepper to taste. Simmer for about 10 minutes.   ❧ ❧ ❧ *The Lady & Sons*

Orange Walnut Salad with Sweet-and-Sour Dressing

SERVES 10 TO 12

SALAD

3 small heads Bibb lettuce, cleaned
and torn into bite-size pieces
1½ pounds fresh spinach, cleaned
and torn into bite-size pieces
3 oranges, peeled, sectioned, and
seeded

¾ medium red onion, sliced and
separated into rings
¾ cup coarsely chopped walnuts
3 teaspoons butter

Combine lettuce, spinach, oranges, and onion in a large bowl. In a saucepan, sauté walnuts in butter until lightly browned. Add to lettuce mixture. Toss with Sweet-and-Sour Dressing.

SWEET-AND-SOUR DRESSING

1½ cups vegetable oil
¾ cup vinegar
¾ cup sugar
1½ teaspoons salt

1½ teaspoons celery seed
1½ teaspoons dry mustard
1½ teaspoons paprika
1½ teaspoons grated onion

Combine all ingredients in a jar. Chill. Shake and serve over salad.

Jamie's Chicken Salad

SERVES 6 TO 8

This is my son Jamie's recipe. It's the best! For a little variation, try adding walnuts and canned mandarin oranges or grapes for a Hawaiian taste.

One 2½- to 3-pound chicken
Salt and pepper to taste
1 onion, quartered
2 ribs plus 1 cup chopped celery
4 hard-boiled eggs, chopped
2 teaspoons Jane's Krazy
   Mixed-Up Salt

½ cup mayonnaise
1 teaspoon lemon-pepper seasoning
¼ teaspoon pepper
2 to 3 tablespoons chicken stock

Put the chicken in a large stockpot along with salt, pepper, onion, and celery stalks. Boil chicken until well done. Reserve stock. Remove chicken from pot. Cool; remove skin and bones. Dice the chicken and combine it with chopped celery and eggs in a large bowl. Add remaining ingredients and mix well.   ❦ ❦ ❦ **The Lady & Sons**

Southern Shrimp Salad

SERVES 6

2 tablespoons (more or less to taste)
   Old Bay Shrimp Boil
2 pounds shrimp, cleaned, peeled,
   and deveined
1 cup uncooked white rice

½ cup chopped onion
½ cup chopped green olives
Pepper to taste
1 cup mayonnaise

Dissolve shrimp boil in 4 cups water and bring to a boil. Add shrimp and boil 4 minutes; drain, reserving shrimp boil water. Chop shrimp into bite-size chunks and put on paper towels; set aside to cool. In the reserved water, boil rice until tender for 15 to 20 minutes; drain rice in colander. Let cool. Add onion, olives, and pepper to rice; stir in mayonnaise. Add cooled, dry shrimp last.   ❦ ❦ ❦ **The Lady & Sons**

Georgia Cracker Salad

SERVES 6

We serve this salad with most of our seafood dishes at the restaurant. It's also quite good at an outdoor fish fry.

1 sleeve saltine crackers
1 large tomato, finely chopped
3 green onions, finely chopped

1½ cups mayonnaise
1 hard-boiled egg, finely chopped

Crush crackers. Mix all ingredients together and serve immediately.

❧ ❧ ❧ **The Lady & Sons**

The Lady's Coleslaw

SERVES APPROXIMATELY 6

To me, the secret to good slaw is the way you cut your cabbage. I have found that I prefer half of the cabbage coarsely chopped in a food processor and half hand-sliced very thin. Use outside dark green leaves, too, for color.

½ bell pepper, chopped
1 green onion, chopped
½ large carrot, chopped
⅛ cup chopped fresh parsley
½ head cabbage
½ cup mayonnaise
½ teaspoon Jane's Krazy
    Mixed-Up Salt

¼ teaspoon coarsely ground black
    pepper
2 tablespoons sugar
¼ teaspoon lemon-pepper seasoning
1 tablespoon white vinegar

In food processor, gently process bell pepper, onion, carrot, and parsley, being careful not to overprocess (don't let mixture become mushy). Cut up half the cabbage into chunks and place in food processor. Process lightly (once again, don't let cabbage become mushy). Thinly slice remaining cabbage. Mix the cabbage together, adding the processed vegetables. Mix remaining ingredients together and allow to stand for a few minutes. Pour over slaw ingredients and toss. Chill for at least an hour. ❧ ❧ ❧ **The Lady & Sons**

Blueberry and Grilled Chicken Salad

SERVES 4

1 head romaine lettuce, chopped
1 cup fresh blueberries
2 oranges, cut into supremes
½ cup feta cheese, crumbled, plus
more for garnish
¼ to ½ cup Poppy Seed Dressing
(see page 127)

2 skinless boneless chicken breasts,
grilled and cut into strips
½ cup glazed slivered almonds
(or plain slivered almonds)

In a large mixing bowl, toss together lettuce, blueberries, orange supremes, feta, and dressing. To serve, place salad in a decorative bowl and top with grilled chicken strips. Sprinkle with almonds and more feta.

The Lady's Warm Potato Salad

SERVES 10 TO 12

8 medium red potatoes
¼ cup chopped fresh parsley
¼ cup chopped green onion tops
1 cup chopped celery
3 hard-boiled eggs, chopped
¼ cup chopped bell pepper
¼ cup diced pimento

1 teaspoon lemon-pepper seasoning
2 tablespoons Jane's Krazy Mixed-
Up Salt
1 tablespoon Dijon mustard
¼ cup mayonnaise
1 cup sour cream

Boil potatoes with skins on for 10 to 15 minutes, until tender. Let cool just to the touch and cut into cubes. In a large bowl, combine remaining ingredients. Add potatoes. Mix gently and serve at room temperature. ❧ ❧ ❧ **The Lady & Sons**

Avocado Chicken Salad

SERVES 8

For a beautiful presentation, I like to cut the avocado in half, carefully scoop the meat from the shell, and then stuff the shell with the chicken salad. Garnish with dressing and a lemon wedge.

3 cups cooked, diced chicken
3 cups cooked white rice
2 avocados, peeled, diced, and
   tossed with 1 tablespoon lemon
   juice (to prevent browning)

¾ cup chopped onion
1 cup mayonnaise
1 to 2 teaspoons pepper
1 teaspoon salt
¼ cup chopped fresh parsley

Mix all ingredients and chill. Pass with avocado dressing.

AVOCADO DRESSING

YIELDS 2 CUPS

1 large avocado, peeled and mashed
   with 2 tablespoons lemon juice
1 cup mayonnaise
½ cup sour cream
½ teaspoon Worcestershire sauce

⅓ cup chopped onion
2 cloves garlic, minced
1 teaspoon salt
Dash of cayenne pepper

Place all ingredients in a food processor and blend until smooth. Chill and serve alongside chicken salad. ❧ ❧ ❧ *The Lady & Sons*

Black-Eyed Pea Salad

SERVES 8

¾ cup olive oil
¼ cup balsamic vinegar
¼ cup sugar
3 cups black-eyed peas, cooked
1 red bell pepper, seeded and diced
½ cup chopped green onion with
    tops
1 large tomato, diced

1 tablespoon minced fresh thyme
1 tablespoon minced fresh rosemary
4 tablespoons minced fresh parsley
2 tablespoons minced fresh oregano
1 large banana pepper (mild),
    seeded and diced
1 hot green pepper, seeded and
    diced (optional)

Mix olive oil, vinegar, and sugar together and pour over the rest of ingredients. Mix well and chill. Use a slotted spoon to serve.

❧ ❧ ❧ *The Lady & Sons*

Esther's Dill Coleslaw

SERVES 6 TO 8

Esther Shaver owns one of the best bookstores in town. Her store, E. Shaver's, was one of the first places to carry my cookbook. Not only is her store great, but so is her coleslaw!

1 small head cabbage, shredded
½ cup finely chopped Vidalia onion
½ cup Hidden Valley Ranch
    Buttermilk salad dressing (made
    as per directions on the dry mix)

½ cup shredded carrots
2 tablespoons chopped fresh dill

Mix all ingredients together except dill. Place slaw in bowl and sprinkle dill on top. Chill and serve.

Peach Pecan Iceberg Wedges

SERVES 6

1 cup pecans, chopped
1 tablespoon butter
½ tablespoon brown sugar
1 cup plain yogurt
2 tablespoons favorite dressing
Juice of ½ lemon

Kosher salt and freshly ground
   pepper to taste
1 head iceberg lettuce, cored and
   cut into 6 wedges
1 fresh peach, very thinly sliced

In a small sauté pan over medium heat, stir together pecans, butter, and brown sugar. Cook until mixture thickens and pecans are coated. Remove from heat and cool. In a small mixing bowl, combine yogurt, dressing, and lemon juice. Salt and pepper to taste. To assemble each salad, arrange 1 lettuce wedge on a beautiful salad plate, top evenly with sliced peaches, and drizzle with yogurt dressing mixture. Garnish with caramelized pecans.

Potato-Egg Salad

SERVES 8 TO 10

6 cups diced new potatoes
⅓ cup Italian salad dressing
1 teaspoon salt
1 cup diced celery
⅓ cup sliced green onions with tops

4 hard-boiled eggs, chopped
1 cup mayonnaise
½ cup sour cream
1 teaspoon dry mustard
½ teaspoon horseradish

Boil potatoes with skins on for 15 to 20 minutes or until tender. Pour salad dressing over warm potatoes. Chill for about 2 hours. Mix remaining ingredients and fold into potato mixture.

Cranberry Salad

SERVES 7 TO 8

One 4-ounce can crushed pineapple
One 3-ounce package black cherry
  Jell-O

6 ounces raw cranberries, rinsed
1 cup broken pecans
½ cup sugar

Drain pineapple and reserve juice. Add juice to ½ cup hot water and heat to boiling. Soften Jell-O in ¼ cup cold water. Dissolve softened Jell-O in hot water–juice mixture. Let cool until it starts to set; *don't let the Jell-O harden.* Put cranberries through a grinder. Add ground berries, pineapple, nuts, and sugar to cooled Jell-O mixture. Mix well. Pour into a bowl or mold. Refrigerate until completely set.

Cornucopia Salad

SERVES 10 TO 12

1 head lettuce (any variety),
  washed, patted dry, and torn
  into pieces
1 cup diced green bell pepper
1 cup diced celery
1 cup frozen green peas (uncooked)
Two 8-ounce cans sliced water
  chestnuts
1 cup fresh chopped mushrooms

3 bananas, sliced and tossed in
  ¼ cup lemon juice
1 cup grated Cheddar cheese
¾ cup raisins
¾ cup chopped nuts (pecans,
  walnuts, or salted peanuts)
¾ cup chopped green onion with
  tops
10 to 12 slices bacon, crisply cooked

DRESSING

2 cups mayonnaise
¼ cup sugar

1 tablespoon white vinegar

In a large rectangular dish, layer salad ingredients in order listed, stopping after bananas. Mix dressing ingredients and let stand for 5 minutes. Frost entire top of salad with dressing, covering it completely. Sprinkle layers of cheese, raisins, and nuts (combined), chopped green onion, and bacon. Chill for 3 to 4 hours before serving.

❧ ❧ ❧ *The Lady & Sons*

Broccoli Salad

SERVES 6 TO 8

1 head broccoli
6 to 8 slices cooked bacon, crumbled
½ cup chopped red onion
½ cup raisins (optional)
8 ounces sharp Cheddar cheese, cut
    into very small chunks

1 cup mayonnaise
2 tablespoons vinegar
¼ cup sugar
1 cup halved cherry tomatoes

Trim off large leaves of broccoli. Remove tough stalks at end and wash broccoli thoroughly. Cut flowerets and stems into bite-size pieces. Place in a large bowl. Add crumbled bacon, onion, raisins, and cheese. In a small bowl, combine remaining ingredients, stirring well. Add to broccoli mixture and toss gently. 🌸 🌸 🌸 **The Lady & Sons**

Roasted Beet Salad

SERVES 6 TO 8

Two 15¼-ounce cans sliced beets,
    rinsed and drained
1½ cups crumbled feta cheese
½ cup pitted ripe olives
¼ cup chopped fresh dill

½ cup olive oil
¼ cup rice wine vinegar
Salt, pepper, and garlic powder
    to taste
Dash of tabasco

Remove broiler tray from oven and coat with nonstick cooking spray. Replace tray and preheat broiler. After beets are drained place on coated broiler tray. Place under hot broiler, turning every 2 to 3 minutes until edges start to brown, approximately 10 to 15 minutes. Remove beets from oven and allow to cool. Mix remaining ingredients with cooled beets. Toss and serve.

Main Courses

MEAT

POULTRY

Low Country Boil

This dish is indigenous to Savannah and our lifestyle. Calling up a dozen friends for a cookout is a great casual way to entertain, especially if the food is cooked outside over an open flame (you can also use a portable gas fish cooker). Once the Low Country Boil has been cooked and drained, I like to pour it out on a table covered with newspaper.

Crab boil (2 teaspoons per quart
   of water)
12 small red new potatoes
Six 4-inch pieces good smoked link
   sausage

6 ears fresh corn
3 pounds fresh shrimp (26 to 30
   count per pound), unpeeled

Fill a large pot with enough water to cover all ingredients. Add crab boil and heat until boiling. Adjust crab boil to suit your taste. When boiling, add potatoes and sausage. Cook on medium heat for 20 minutes. Add corn and cook for an additional 10 minutes. Add shrimp and cook for no more than 3 minutes (do not overcook!). Drain and serve with piping-hot bread and ice-cold beer.   ❦ ❦ ❦   *The Lady & Sons*

Black Pepper Shrimp

3 pounds fresh shrimp, unpeeled
8 tablespoons (1 stick) butter
2 to 3 tablespoons chopped garlic

4 tablespoons freshly ground black
   pepper

Preheat oven to 450 degrees. Wash and drain shrimp. Place in a shallow baking pan. Melt butter in a saucepan. Add garlic and sauté 3 to 4 minutes. Pour over shrimp and toss to coat. Pepper shrimp until shrimp are covered well. Bake until pink (about 5 minutes), turn, bake a few minutes longer, and pepper again. This will not be good unless you use a heavy hand with the pepper. Serve with a fresh garden salad and hot French bread. Dip bread in the pan juices for an extra treat.

❦ ❦ ❦   *The Lady & Sons*

Savory Salmon

SERVES 4

One 2-pound salmon fillet
House Seasoning (see page 180)
Juice of 2 lemons
1 medium orange, sectioned and
 seeded
1 medium onion, sliced thin
1 small red bell pepper, julienned
1 small green bell pepper, julienned

1 pint strawberries, cleaned and
 sliced
½ cup water
½ cup honey
½ cup chopped fresh chervil or
 baby dill
4 cloves garlic, minced
1 bunch chives, chopped

Preheat oven to 350 degrees. Place salmon fillet on a foil-lined pan. Season with House Seasoning and lemon juice, then cover and surround fish with orange, onion, and red and green bell pepper. Mix strawberries, water, honey, chervil or dill, garlic, and chives together. Pour evenly over salmon. Cover with foil and pierce foil, allowing salmon to steam. Bake for 25 to 30 minutes. Serve with rice.

Savannah Crab Cakes

SERVES 4 TO 6

1 pound crabmeat, picked free
 of shell
½ cup crushed Ritz crackers
3 green onions, finely chopped, with
 tops
½ cup finely chopped bell pepper
¼ cup mayonnaise
1 egg

1 teaspoon Worcestershire sauce
1 teaspoon dry mustard
Juice of ½ lemon
¼ teaspoon garlic powder
1 teaspoon salt
Dash of cayenne pepper
Flour for dusting
½ cup peanut oil

Mix all ingredients together except flour and peanut oil. Shape into patties and dust with flour. Panfry in hot peanut oil over medium heat until browned, for 4 to 5 minutes. Flip and panfry other side until golden brown.

TARTAR SAUCE

½ cup chopped green onion
½ cup chopped dill pickle
1 cup mayonnaise

½ teaspoon House Seasoning
(see page 180)

In a bowl, combine chopped onion, pickle, mayonnaise, and House Seasoning and mix well. Serve alongside crab cakes with lemon wedges.

❧ ❧ ❧ *The Lady & Sons*

VARIATION: Substitute ⅓ cup capers for ½ cup pickles and add a dash of cayenne pepper.

Spicy Shrimp and Pasta Casserole

SERVES 8

2 eggs
1½ cups half-and-half
1 cup plain yogurt
½ cup grated Swiss cheese
⅓ cup crumbled feta cheese
⅓ cup chopped fresh parsley
1 teaspoon dried basil, crushed

1 teaspoon dried oregano, crushed
9 ounces angel hair pasta, cooked
16 ounces mild salsa, thick and
*   chunky*
2 pounds shrimp, cleaned, peeled,
*   and deveined*
½ cup grated Monterey Jack cheese

Preheat oven to 350 degrees. Grease a 12 × 8-inch pan or glass dish with butter. Combine eggs, half-and-half, yogurt, Swiss and feta cheeses, parsley, basil, and oregano in medium bowl; mix well. Spread half the pasta on bottom of prepared pan. Cover with salsa. Add half of the shrimp. Cover with Monterey Jack cheese. Cover with remaining pasta and shrimp. Spread egg mixture over top. Bake for 30 minutes or until bubbly. Let stand for 10 minutes.

Scallops Charleston

SERVES 4

1½ pounds fresh sea scallops
Salt and pepper to taste
½ teaspoon garlic powder
¼ teaspoon paprika
¼ cup finely chopped fresh basil
Flour for dusting
¾ cup sherry or dry white wine

1 shallot, finely chopped
8 ounces fresh mushrooms,
*   quartered*
2 tablespoons butter
3 tablespoons all-purpose flour
1 cup grated Gruyère cheese

Season scallops with salt, pepper, garlic powder, paprika, and basil. Dust scallops with flour. Sauté in a pan that has been lightly coated with nonstick cooking spray and a small amount of olive oil. Cook scallops on both sides until browned. Remove scallops from pan. To the drippings in the pan, add sherry, shallots, and mushrooms; cook for approximately 3 to 4 minutes. In a separate saucepan, melt butter over medium heat and add 3 tablespoons flour. Mix well and cook for 2 minutes over low heat, stirring constantly. Pour shallots, mushrooms, and liquid from scallops into flour mixture. Mix well. Stir scallops into sauce. (If too thick, you can thin with clam juice or fish or chicken stock.) Transfer to four individual baking dishes, top with cheese, and broil for 1 minute, until browned. Serve with wild rice.

Southern Fried Oysters
with Spicy Dipping Sauce

SERVES 4

⅓ cup Paula Deen Vidalia Onion
*   Peach Grilling Marinade*
1 tablespoon sour cream
½ cup all-purpose flour
2 large eggs
3 tablespoons The Lady & Sons
*   Signature Hot Sauce*

1 cup panko bread crumbs
12 oysters, freshly shucked
2 cups peanut oil (or canola oil)
Kosher salt

To prepare dipping sauce, in a small bowl, combine marinade and sour cream. Mix well and set aside. Place flour in a small bowl. Whisk eggs and hot sauce in a second small bowl. Place bread crumbs in a third small bowl. Dredge oysters in flour, shaking off any excess. Dip flour-dredged oysters in egg mixture, shaking off any excess. Roll oysters in bread crumbs, coating completely. Place on baking sheet and place in refrigerator while frying oil comes to temperature. In a heavy skillet, heat oil to 325 degrees. Add breaded oysters and fry until golden brown, about 1 to 2 minutes. Drain on paper towels and immediately sprinkle with salt. Serve warm with dipping sauce.

Deviled Seafood Casserole

SERVES 8

1½ pounds shrimp, cleaned, peeled, and deveined
1 pound fresh sea scallops
12 tablespoons (1½ sticks) butter
One 1-pound haddock fillet
½ cup plus 1 tablespoon all-purpose flour
1 cup evaporated milk
1 cup consommé or beef broth
2 tablespoons cornstarch
⅓ cup milk

1 teaspoon garlic powder
1 tablespoon horseradish
½ teaspoon salt
1 teaspoon soy sauce
2 tablespoons chopped fresh parsley
1 tablespoon Worcestershire sauce
1 teaspoon dry mustard
¼ teaspoon cayenne pepper
1 tablespoon lemon juice
4 teaspoons ketchup
½ cup sherry

Preheat oven to 400 degrees. Sauté shrimp and scallops in 4 tablespoons butter for 3 to 5 minutes, until tender. In a saucepan, steam fish in small amount of water for 3 minutes, until tender, and cut into bite-size pieces. In a saucepan, melt remaining 8 tablespoons butter; add flour and evaporated milk; mix and add consommé. Cook over medium heat until thick. Mix cornstarch in ⅓ cup of milk and add remaining ingredients except sherry. Add to sauce and stir well. Add seafood and stir in sherry. Pour into a casserole and bake for 30 minutes.

Mushroom-Stuffed Baked Red Snapper

SERVES 4

½ pound fresh mushrooms, or one
    8-ounce can stems and pieces
4 tablespoons (½ stick) butter
½ cup finely chopped celery
5 tablespoons minced onion
One 8-ounce can water chestnuts,
    drained and chopped
½ cup soft bread crumbs
1 egg, lightly beaten

1 tablespoon soy sauce
1 tablespoon chopped fresh parsley
Salt and pepper to taste
Two 2½-pound oven-ready whole
    red snappers, gutted, scaled,
    and cleaned
½ cup dry white wine
¾ cup water

Preheat oven to 350 degrees. Rinse, pat dry, and finely chop ¼ pound mushrooms. Quarter remaining mushrooms or drain canned mushrooms. Set aside. In a small skillet, melt 2 tablespoons butter; add celery and 3 tablespoons of the onion. Sauté for 5 minutes. Combine sautéed celery mixture with mushrooms, water chestnuts, bread crumbs, egg, soy sauce, parsley, and salt and pepper. Mix well and spoon into fish cavities. Secure openings with skewers or toothpicks. Sprinkle both sides of each fish with salt and pepper. Place in a large baking dish. Dot with remaining 2 tablespoons of butter, 2 tablespoons onion, the wine, and water. Bake uncovered for 45 to 50 minutes. Baste occasionally. Test with a fork. When fish flakes, it's done.

Peel and Eat Shrimp

SERVES 4 TO 6

3 tablespoons crab boil seasoning
2 pounds large shrimp, shells on

1 lemon, sliced into wedges
Cocktail sauce (see recipe facing)

In a large pot, bring 8 cups of water and crab boil seasoning to a boil and stir in shrimp. Remove from heat, cover, and let stand for 15 minutes, until shrimp turn pink. Drain and serve with lemon wedges and cocktail sauce.

COCKTAIL SAUCE

YIELDS 2½ CUPS

2 cups ketchup
¼ cup prepared horseradish
2 tablespoons Worcestershire sauce
1 tablespoon The Lady & Sons
   Signature Hot Sauce

Juice of 1 lemon
½ teaspoon black pepper

In a bowl, combine all ingredients. Cover and chill until ready to serve. Store in a sealed container or squeeze bottle and refrigerate for up to one week.

Shrimp and Scallop Fraîche

SERVES 4

½ cup crème fraîche
1 pound shrimp, cleaned, peeled,
   and deveined
1 pound fresh sea scallops
4 tablespoons (½ stick) butter
Juice of 1 lemon

3 cloves garlic, minced
1 tablespoon cognac or wine
1 tablespoon cornstarch
2 tablespoons fish or chicken stock
4 sprigs fresh basil

CRÈME FRAÎCHE

1 cup heavy cream

2 tablespoons sour cream

Prepare crème fraîche ahead of time by combining heavy cream and sour cream. Cover with plastic wrap and let stand at room temperature for 12 to 24 hours. Clean and devein shrimp, leaving tails on. Pat scallops dry with paper towels. Melt butter in a large skillet. Add lemon juice and garlic. Place shrimp and scallops in butter and sauté until scallops are opaque, 3 to 4 minutes per side. Remove to a warm platter. Add cognac or wine to pan juice. Dissolve cornstarch in stock and add along with crème fraîche to pan. Simmer until thickened. Pour sauce over shellfish and garnish with basil sprigs.

Fillet of Sole Paprika

SERVES 3 TO 4

1½ pounds fillet of sole
1 onion, sliced thin
1 cup sour cream
⅓ cup white table wine

1 tablespoon all-purpose flour
Juice of ½ lemon
½ teaspoon paprika
Salt and pepper to taste

Preheat oven to 375 degrees. Arrange fillets in a greased shallow baking dish. Cover with onion slices. Blend sour cream, wine, flour, lemon juice, and seasonings and pour over entire baking dish. Bake for about 25 minutes, or until fish is tender.

Shrimp with Rice

SERVES 8

Two 6-ounce boxes Uncle Ben's
    long-grain and wild rice
2 pounds shrimp, cleaned, peeled,
    and deveined
1 onion, diced and sautéed in 2
    tablespoons butter
1 bell pepper, chopped

Two 10¾-ounce cans condensed
    cream of mushroom soup
16 ounces grated Cheddar cheese;
    reserve ½ cup for top
1 tablespoon Worcestershire sauce
½ teaspoon dry mustard

Remove seasoning mix from rice; do not use. Cook rice as directed on box. Preheat oven to 375 degrees. Mix rice with remaining ingredients in a baking dish and sprinkle reserved cheese on top. Bake for 45 minutes.

Shrimp Gumbo Casserole

SERVES 6

This Southern dish usually is prepared and served in an iron skillet, but may be cooked in a frying pan with an ovenproof handle.

1 cup finely chopped onion
1 cup finely chopped celery
2 tablespoons olive oil
One 14½-ounce can diced tomatoes
2 bay leaves
½ teaspoon dried thyme
One 10-ounce package frozen
   cut okra

1 teaspoon lemon-pepper seasoning
1½ teaspoons House Seasoning
   (see page 180)
1 cup chicken or fish stock
2 cups shrimp, cleaned, peeled,
   and deveined

In an iron skillet sauté onion and celery in oil. Add tomatoes, bay leaves, thyme, okra, lemon-pepper seasoning, and House Seasoning. Pour in stock. Cover pot and gently simmer for 30 minutes. Remove from heat and stir in shrimp. Prepare topping.

TOPPING

1 egg, beaten
⅓ cup milk

One 12-ounce package corn
   muffin mix

Preheat oven to 400 degrees. Mix together egg and milk. In separate bowl, place muffin mix and add egg-milk mixture. Mix until just well blended. Drop by tablespoonfuls on top of hot shrimp mixture, leaving the center uncovered. Bake 15 to 20 minutes.

Lemon Mackerel

SERVES 4

2 pounds Spanish mackerel fillets,
   skin on
¼ cup olive oil
½ cup lemon juice

2 tablespoons butter
1 teaspoon salt
1 teaspoon lemon-pepper seasoning
Lemon slices

Preheat oven to 350 degrees. Rinse fish fillets and lay on paper towels to dry. Rub a glass casserole dish with olive oil. Also rub fish fillets with olive oil. Lay fillets skin side down in dish. Pour lemon juice on fish (¼ inch in dish) and spread fish with butter. Sprinkle with salt and lemon-pepper seasoning. Put about three slices of lemon on each fillet. Bake for 20 to 30 minutes, until fish flakes easily with fork. If you would like your fillet to brown more, put it under the broiler for 2 to 3 extra minutes.

Shrimp and Mushroom Casserole

SERVES 4

This recipe can be served as a main dish with a green salad and French bread or as a side dish with steak or seafood.

8 tablespoons (1 stick) butter
¾ cup all-purpose flour
1½ cups half-and-half
One 10¾-ounce can condensed
   cream of mushroom soup
One 13¼-ounce can sliced
   mushrooms, drained

½ cup grated Parmesan cheese
1 pound cooked shrimp, peeled,
   deveined, and coarsely diced
Garlic powder
Buttered bread crumbs for topping

Preheat oven to 350 degrees. In saucepan over medium heat, melt butter and stir in flour, then slowly blend in half-and-half, stirring constantly. Sauce will be thick. Do not brown. Add mushroom soup, sliced mushrooms, and Parmesan cheese. Fold in shrimp. Add garlic powder to taste. Pour mixture into buttered casserole dish and top with buttered bread crumbs. Bake for 25 to 30 minutes.

Oven-Fried Catfish

SERVES 4

4 catfish fillets
Salt and black pepper
1 cup buttermilk
2 tablespoons The Lady & Sons
    Signature Hot Sauce

2 tablespoons olive oil
1 cup yellow cornmeal
1 cup flour
2 teaspoons crab boil seasoning

Season catfish filets on both sides with salt and pepper. Mix together buttermilk and hot sauce in an 8 × 8-inch casserole dish. Add catfish fillets, making sure they're completely covered by liquid. Let sit for 15 minutes. Meanwhile, preheat oven to 475 degrees. Coat a sheet tray with olive oil. Place in the oven and heat while you prep the remaining ingredients. In a second casserole dish, whisk together cornmeal, flour, and crab boil seasoning. Remove catfish filets from buttermilk, letting excess drip off, and dredge catfish on both sides in the cornmeal mixture. Transfer to the hot sheet tray. Bake for 6 minutes, then carefully flip catfish and continue cooking for 5 minutes more, or until cooked through and golden.

Red Snapper Stuffed with Crabmeat

SERVES 8

1 whole dressed red snapper, at least 7 pounds	*2 eggs, beaten*
Salt and pepper to taste	*1 medium onion, chopped*
Garlic powder to taste	*1 sleeve saltine crackers, crushed*
Onion salt to taste	*6 slices bacon*
2 pounds crabmeat, picked free of shell	*2 slices lemon*
	¼ teaspoon dried dill or 1 tablespoon chopped fresh dill

Preheat oven to 350 degrees. Line a baking pan with aluminum foil. Grease the foil so the fish won't stick. Lay the fish in the pan. Season inside and out with salt, pepper, garlic powder, and onion salt. Make two slits on the side of the fish facing up. To stuff the fish, mix the crabmeat, beaten eggs, chopped onion, saltines, salt, and pepper to taste. Stuff this mixture in the cavity of the fish. If it is more than the fish will hold, put it all around the cavity. Lay bacon and lemon slices on fish and lightly sprinkle with dill. Bake, covered, for 1 hour. Remove cover for the last few minutes to brown.

Shrimp and Artichoke Bake

SERVES 4

2 tablespoons butter
2 tablespoons all-purpose flour
1½ cups half-and-half
¼ cup grated Parmesan cheese
¼ cup sherry
1 tablespoon Worcestershire sauce
1 teaspoon House Seasoning (see
    page 180)
2 egg yolks, lightly beaten

One 13¾-ounce can artichoke
    hearts, drained and chopped
1 pound shrimp, cleaned, peeled,
    and deveined
¼ pound fresh mushrooms
¾ cup grated Cheddar and
    Monterey Jack cheese
    (combined)
Paprika to taste

Preheat oven to 350 degrees. Melt butter in saucepan over medium heat. Blend in flour to make a paste. Add half-and-half all at once, stirring constantly until thickened and smooth. Add Parmesan cheese, sherry, Worcestershire sauce, and garlic powder, salt, and pepper. Temper egg yolks with 2 tablespoons of hot mixture and add back to remaining cheese sauce. Set aside. Mix artichoke hearts, shrimp, and mushrooms together. Put in baking dish and pour sauce over top. Sprinkle top with grated cheese and paprika. Bake for 30 to 35 minutes. Serve over rice.

Bourbon Beef Tenderloin

SERVES 8 TO 10

This recipe is for the grill. Beef can also be cooked in the oven at 350 degrees for 45 minutes to 1 hour. Use a meat thermometer: rare—115 to 120 degrees; medium rare—130 to 135 degrees; medium—140 to 145 degrees. Buy a whole tenderloin, about 4½ to 5 pounds, and have the butcher remove the "silver" connective tissue.

1 cup bourbon	2 cups water
1 cup brown sugar	3 to 4 sprigs fresh thyme, chopped
⅔ cup soy sauce	1 beef tenderloin, silver connective
1 bunch cilantro, chopped	tissue removed
½ cup lemon juice	Oil for grill
1 tablespoon Worcestershire sauce	

Prepare marinade by combining bourbon, brown sugar, soy sauce, cilantro, lemon juice, Worcestershire sauce, water, and thyme. Be sure tenderloin is completely trimmed of any fat and connective tissue. Fold the tail end of the beef back underneath itself so that it is of uniform thickness. Secure with butcher's string. Pour marinade over meat, cover, and refrigerate 8 to 12 hours. Turn meat over several times during that time. Prepare grill for cooking (or preheat oven to 350 degrees). When fire is ready, place meat on oiled grill, reserving marinade. Cook over high heat with lid closed, turning often; occasionally baste. Cooks rare in about 30 or 45 minutes in the oven. Serve with Horseradish Cream on the side.

HORSERADISH CREAM

1 cup heavy cream	¼ cup horseradish, drained

Whip cream until stiff. Stir in horseradish, mixing well.

Old-Time Beef Stew

SERVES 6

2 pounds stew beef
2 tablespoons vegetable oil
2 cups water
1 teaspoon Worcestershire sauce
1 clove garlic, peeled
1 or 2 bay leaves
1 medium onion, sliced
1 teaspoon salt
1 teaspoon sugar

½ teaspoon pepper
½ teaspoon paprika
Dash of ground allspice or ground
    cloves
3 large carrots, sliced
4 red potatoes, quartered
3 ribs celery, chopped
2 tablespoons cornstarch

Brown meat in hot oil. Add water, Worcestershire sauce, garlic, bay leaves, onion, salt, sugar, pepper, paprika, and allspice. Cover and simmer 1½ hours. Remove bay leaves and garlic clove. Add carrots, potatoes, and celery. Cover and cook 30 to 40 minutes longer. To thicken gravy, remove 2 cups hot liquid. Using a separate bowl, combine ¼ cup water and cornstarch until smooth. Mix with hot liquid and return mixture to pot. Stir and cook until bubbly.   ❦ ❦ ❦ *The Lady & Sons*

Barbecue-Style Pork Chops

SERVES 6

6 center-cut pork chops, trimmed
    of fat
1 tablespoon vegetable oil
One 14½-ounce can whole
    tomatoes, crushed

½ cup ketchup
¼ cup dark brown sugar
2 tablespoons Worcestershire sauce
2 tablespoons prepared mustard
½ teaspoon salt

Preheat oven to 350 degrees. Brown pork chops in oil. Drain, then place in a 13 × 9-inch baking dish. Combine remaining ingredients and spoon over chops. Bake for 45 minutes. Great served with macaroni and cheese!

Basic Meat Loaf

SERVES 4

1 pound ground beef
1¼ teaspoons salt
¼ teaspoon ground black pepper
½ cup chopped onion
½ cup chopped bell pepper

1 egg, lightly beaten
8 ounces canned diced tomatoes,
   with juice
½ cup quick-cooking oats

Preheat oven to 375 degrees. Mix all meat loaf ingredients well and place in a baking dish. Shape into a loaf.

TOPPING

⅓ cup ketchup
2 tablespoons brown sugar

1 tablespoon prepared mustard

Mix ingredients for topping and spread on loaf. Bake for 1 hour.

❦ ❦ ❦ **The Lady & Sons**

Pot Roast

SERVES 6

Put this on to cook in a Crock-Pot before leaving for work and come home in the evening to a mouthwatering dinner.

One 3-pound boneless chuck roast
1½ teaspoons House Seasoning (see
   page 180)
¼ cup vegetable oil
1 onion, thinly sliced
3 bay leaves

3 or 4 beef bouillon cubes, crushed
2 cloves garlic, crushed
One 10¾-ounce can condensed
   cream of mushroom soup
¼ to ½ cup Chardonnay wine

Sprinkle roast on all sides with House Seasoning; season well. In moderately hot skillet, brown roast on all sides in oil. Place roast in Crock-Pot. On top of the roast, layer onion, bay leaves, crushed beef bouillon cubes, crushed garlic, and cream of mushroom soup. Add Chardonnay. Cover with just enough water to cover all the ingredients sufficiently. Cook on low setting approximately 8 hours.

Easy Grilled Baby Back Ribs

SERVES 4

*1 tablespoon freshly ground black
  pepper*
1 tablespoon chili powder
2 tablespoons paprika
*2 tablespoons packed dark brown
  sugar*

2 teaspoons garlic powder
¾ teaspoon salt
*2 pounds baby back ribs
  (about 2 racks), back
  membranes removed*

In a small bowl, stir together all ingredients except ribs and set aside. Using your fingers, rub spice mixture over ribs to coat evenly. Place each rack of ribs in large resealable bag. Refrigerate overnight, turning bag occasionally. (If ribs will not fit in bag, place on baking sheet and wrap well with plastic wrap.) Prepare grill for medium direct heat. Remove ribs from plastic bag and wrap each rack separately in double layer of heavy-duty foil. Grill, covered, for 25 minutes. Turn packets over and grill for 25 minutes more. Test for doneness by poking fork between bones: meat should be very tender. If ribs are not done, return to grill and cook for 10 to 15 minutes more, or until fork tender. Carefully remove packets from grill. Unwrap ribs and place directly on grill; cook for 2 to 3 minutes per side, or until crisp. Transfer ribs to cutting board. Let stand for 10 minutes before cutting into individual ribs.

Pepper Steak

SERVES 4

One 1½-pound round steak
Sprinkle of paprika
2 tablespoons butter
Garlic salt to taste
One 10½-ounce can beef broth

1 large onion
1 large bell pepper
2 tablespoons cornstarch
¼ cup water
¼ cup soy sauce

Pound round steak and cut into ¼-inch strips; sprinkle with paprika. Brown meat in butter; add garlic salt and beef broth. Cover; simmer for 30 minutes. Cut onion and pepper into strips. Add to meat and simmer for 5 minutes. Mix cornstarch, water, and soy sauce and add to meat mixture. Simmer until sauce thickens slightly. Serve over rice.

❦ ❦ ❦ *The Lady & Sons*

Burgundy Beef Roast

YIELD DEPENDS ON SIZE OF ROAST (6 TO 8 OUNCES PER SERVING)

1 eye of round roast (be sure you
    know exact weight)
½ cup red Burgundy wine

⅓ cup soy sauce
2 tablespoons cracked black pepper

Place roast in glass container large enough to hold it comfortably. Make marinade of Burgundy wine, soy sauce, and pepper. Pour over meat and marinate overnight. Next day, place roast in shallow pan with just a little of the marinade. Preheat oven to 500 degrees. Cook uncovered for 5 minutes per pound of meat. Turn off oven and cover roast with foil. Leave in oven for 40 minutes for medium-rare roast. Let cool and slice very thin.

Beef Stroganoff

SERVES 4 TO 6

6 tablespoons all-purpose flour
⅔ cup water
4 tablespoons (½ stick) butter
2 pounds round steak
1 teaspoon House Seasoning
    (see page 180)

One 10¾-ounce can condensed
    cream of mushroom soup
One 10¾-ounce can condensed
    French onion soup
1 cup sour cream

Mix flour and water and set aside. Heat butter in a large, heavy skillet. Season steak with House Seasoning and cook until brown on both sides. Remove from pan and cut into thin strips. Add to pan drippings cream of mushroom soup, French onion soup, 1 soup can water, and flour mixture. Simmer and stir constantly until thickened (if too thick, add a small amount of water). Add steak and simmer for 45 minutes. Add sour cream and heat until bubbling. Serve over cooked noodles.

❧ ❧ ❧ *The Lady & Sons*

Baked Pork Chops

SERVES 4

Four 8-ounce bone-in pork chops,
    about 1 inch thick
1¼ teaspoons salt
1¼ teaspoons freshly ground black
    pepper
3 teaspoons garlic powder
1 pinch cayenne pepper

1 pinch celery seed
½ cup all-purpose flour
3 large eggs, beaten
1 tablespoon Dijon mustard
1 cup panko bread crumbs
¼ cup Parmesan cheese
1 teaspoon dried parsley

Preheat oven to 425 degrees. Season each pork chop on both sides with salt, black pepper, garlic powder, cayenne pepper, and celery seeds. Place flour in a large shallow dish. In a second shallow dish, whisk together eggs and mustard. In a third shallow dish, combine bread crumbs, Parmesan cheese, and parsley. Dip each pork chop into flour and coat well, then dip into egg mixture, shaking off any excess, and finally dip into bread crumbs, patting on crumbs if necessary. Bake pork chops on a wire rack set over a baking sheet for 20 to 25 minutes.

Sausage-Rice Casserole

SERVES 4

One 6-ounce box Uncle Ben's
  long-grain and wild rice
1 pound ground sausage
2 small onions, chopped

One 4-ounce can mushroom pieces
One 10¾-ounce can condensed
  cream of mushroom soup
4 tablepoons (½ stick) butter

Preheat oven to 350 degrees. Cook rice according to directions on box. In a heavy skillet over medium heat, cook sausage until thoroughly done, about 4 to 5 minutes; drain. Combine all ingredients except butter and pour into casserole dish. Dot top with butter. Bake until bubbly, about 25 minutes.   ❧ ❧ ❧ **The Lady & Sons**

Cheeseburger Meat Loaf and Sauce

SERVES 6 TO 8

2 pounds ground beef
2 teaspoons House Seasoning
  (see page 180)
1 medium onion, chopped
1 medium bell pepper, chopped
1 cup grated Cheddar cheese

¼ cup Worcestershire sauce
1 cup sour cream
1 cup crushed Ritz crackers
1 teaspoon Lawry's Seasoned Salt
8 to 10 slices white bread

Preheat oven to 325 degrees. Mix all ingredients except bread slices well. Shape into loaf. Place loaf on 1-inch-deep jelly roll pan lined with white bread slices. Bake loaf for 45 to 60 minutes. The bread absorbs the grease and should be discarded after loaf is removed from oven.

SAUCE

One 10¾-ounce can condensed
  cream of mushroom soup

1 soup-can measure of milk
1½ cups grated Cheddar cheese

Heat soup and milk over medium heat; add cheese. Pour over meat loaf or pass at the table.   ❧ ❧ ❧ **The Lady & Sons**

Roast Prime Rib of Beef with Rich Pan Sauce

SERVES 6

12-pound prime rib roast
2 tablespoons House Seasoning
(see page 180)
2 cups beef stock (or canned beef broth)

1 sprig fresh thyme, or ½ teaspoon dried thyme
2 tablespoons Paula Deen Whiskey Wine Steak Sauce
Salt and black pepper to taste

Preheat oven to 425 degrees. Rub roast with House Seasoning. Place roast in a roasting pan, fat side up, so ribs act as rack. Roast for 30 minutes; reduce heat to 350 degrees. Continue to roast for 2 hours, or until internal temperature on meat thermometer registers your desired doneness. Transfer to a platter and let rest for 15 minutes. While roast is resting, prepare pan sauce. Skim off fat from pan drippings. Place roasting pan over medium heat and add beef stock and thyme. Bring to a boil and simmer for 5 minutes. Whisk in steak sauce. Salt and pepper to taste. Serve warm alongside prime rib roast.

NOTE: A kitchen thermometer indicates doneness: 115 to 120 degrees is rare, 130 to 135 degrees is medium rare, 140 to 145 degrees is medium, and 160 degrees is well done.

Ham Fried Rice with Pineapple

SERVES 8

3 tablespoons vegetable oil
1 small onion, diced
2 tablespoons minced garlic
2 tablespoons minced ginger
4 cups cooked white rice
1 teaspoon salt
2 cups diced leftover ham
One 20-ounce can pineapple rings,
   cut into bite-size pieces
1 cup frozen peas, thawed

¼ cup soy sauce, plus more
   for garnish
2 tablespoons apple cider vinegar
3 tablespoons The Lady & Sons
   Signature Hot Sauce
4 eggs
4 scallions, sliced on bias,
   for garnish
¼ cup fresh cilantro leaves,
   for garnish

In a wok or large skillet, heat vegetable oil. Add onion, garlic, and ginger. Cook until golden. Add rice and fry until coated with oil and slightly golden. Add salt, ham, pineapple, peas, soy sauce, vinegar, and hot sauce. Toss and cook 2 to 3 minutes. In a separate skillet, fry eggs at medium heat, sunny-side up, or to your liking. Spread fried rice onto a platter and place fried eggs on top. Garnish with scallions, cilantro, and drizzle of soy sauce.

Veal and Creamed Spinach

SERVES 4 TO 6

4 to 6 veal scallopini
1 egg, beaten
1 teaspoon House Seasoning
  (see page 180)
1 sleeve from one 16-ounce box Ritz
  crackers, crushed
3 tablespoons olive oil

½ cup white wine
1 large onion, chopped
1 bunch fresh spinach, trimmed at
  stems, soaked, and cleaned
  thoroughly
¼ cup heavy cream (optional)
Salt and pepper to taste

Between sheets of wax paper, pound veal into ¼-inch-thick slices. Beat egg with House Seasoning. Dip veal in egg, then dip into Ritz cracker crumbs. Sauté in heated oil for about 2 minutes on each side over medium heat. Pour wine into pan and cook for another minute or two. Remove veal. Add chopped onion and fresh spinach to pan and sauté until spinach is done, 2 to 3 minutes (don't overcook). Add cream and continue to sauté for 1 more minute or until hot. Season with salt and pepper. Pour onto platter. Place veal on top of spinach. Garnish as you wish and serve from the platter at the table. If you're looking to cut back on calories, don't add the cream.

Foolproof Standing Rib Roast

SERVES 6 TO 8

One 5-pound standing rib roast   *1 tablespoon House Seasoning*
                                       (see page 180)

Follow this method for a rib roast that is lusciously browned on the outside and rare on the inside—regardless of size. Allow roast to stand at room temperature for at least 1 hour. If roast is frozen, thaw completely; bring to room temperature. Preheat oven to 375 degrees. Rub roast with House Seasoning; place roast on rack in pan—rib side down, fatty side up. Roast for 1 hour. Turn off oven. Leave roast in oven but *do not open oven door.* Thirty to 40 minutes before serving time, turn oven to 375 degrees and reheat roast. Important: Do not remove roast or open oven door from time roast is put in until ready to serve.

❧ ❧ ❧ **The Lady & Sons**

Savannah Sloppy Joes

SERVES 8

3 pounds ground beef
1 cup chopped sweet onion
½ cup chopped green pepper
6 tablespoons all-purpose flour
12 ounces The Lady's Barbecue
* Sauce (see page 124)*

2 tablespoons Paula Deen
* Collection Vidalia Onion*
* Steak Sauce*
Salt and black pepper to taste
8 sandwich buns, split and toasted
8 slices American cheese

Cook ground beef, onion, and green pepper until beef is no longer red, stirring to break up. Sprinkle flour over beef; stir to blend thoroughly. Add barbecue sauce and steak sauce and simmer, stirring often, for 15 to 25 minutes, or until thickened. If mixture becomes too thick, add warm water to thin out. Season with salt and black pepper to taste. To serve, top toasted bun with large scoop of hot sloppy joe mixture and single slice of cheese.

Swiss Steak

SERVES 4

*1 round steak (approximately
1½ pounds) (see Note)*
1 teaspoon garlic powder
Salt and pepper to taste
Flour for dusting
⅓ cup vegetable oil

2 cloves garlic, crushed
*One 14½-ounce can diced
tomatoes*
1 medium onion, cut into strips
*1 medium bell pepper, cut into
strips*

Cut steak into serving-size pieces. Season to taste with garlic powder and salt and pepper. Dust meat with flour. In heavy skillet, brown both sides of meat in vegetable oil. Transfer to Dutch oven. Combine garlic, tomatoes, onion, bell pepper, and 1 tomato-can measure of water. Pour over steak and simmer until meat is tender. Season to taste with additional salt and pepper. Hint: This is good to cook in Crock-Pot on low for a most fabulous dinner.

NOTE: To ensure tenderness, it is necessary to have the butcher run the round steak through a cuber.

Farmer's Pork Chops

SERVES 8

8 medium potatoes
½ medium onion
Salt and pepper to taste
White sauce (see recipe below; you
   may also use your own)

1 cup all-purpose flour
2 tablespoons Lawry's Seasoned Salt
8 center-cut pork chops, about
   ½ inch thick
⅓ cup vegetable oil

Preheat oven to 350 degrees. Peel potatoes; slice ¼ inch thick and cover with cold water. Slice onion into very thin slices. Cut slices in half. Drain potatoes; layer half the potatoes in a well-greased 15 × 10-inch casserole dish. Sprinkle with salt and pepper to taste. Scatter half of onion slices on top of potatoes. Repeat with remaining potatoes and onions. Cover potatoes with white sauce. Cover casserole dish with plastic wrap and microwave for 5 minutes on high or bake uncovered for 15 minutes. Mix together flour and seasoned salt and dredge pork chops in flour mixture. Lightly brown chops in vegetable oil. *Do not cook them completely.* As chops are removed from frying pan, lay them on top of potatoes. Bake at 350 degrees for 45 to 60 minutes. The juices from the pork chops will drip down into the potatoes. Delicious!

WHITE SAUCE

8 tablespoons (1 stick) butter
½ cup all-purpose flour
1 to 2 teaspoons salt
½ to ¾ teaspoon pepper

4 cups milk
¼ cup chopped fresh parsley or
   chives (optional)

Melt butter; remove from heat. Stir in flour; add salt and pepper. Return to heat and cook, stirring constantly, until mixture is bubbly. Add milk, 1 cup at a time. Bring to a boil over medium heat, stirring frequently. Reduce heat and simmer 1 to 2 minutes, then let stand at least 1 to 2 minutes. Stir in parsley or chives, if desired.

Steak and Greens

SERVES 6

For the best flavor, you must use at least three types of greens—turnip, collard, mustard, and spinach are all good. When you brown the flour, you should stir it about five minutes. (I always keep a batch in the fridge.)

1½ pounds beef flank or round
   steak, sliced thin
2 tablespoons vegetable oil
2 cups chopped onion
12 to 15 cups greens, washed and
   chopped

6 cups beef stock
5 tablespoons all-purpose flour,
   browned in hot, dry skillet

SEASONING MIX

1 tablespoon paprika
2 teaspoons salt
2 teaspoons dry mustard
1½ teaspoons onion powder
1 teaspoon garlic powder
1 teaspoon dried thyme

¾ teaspoon white pepper
½ teaspoon ground black pepper
¼ teaspoon cayenne pepper
½ teaspoon ground cumin
1 teaspoon ground ginger

Mix together seasoning mix. Sprinkle 2 tablespoons on sliced steak, tossing to insure the meat is covered. (Set aside remaining seasoning for later use.) Heat heavy 5-quart pot; add oil. Brown seasoned meat 2 or 3 minutes, turning once. Add onion, rest of seasoning mix, and ½ cup of each type of greens. Cook, scraping bottom of pot to clear all brown bits, for 5 to 10 minutes. Add 1 cup stock, cover, and cook for 15 minutes. Add browned flour and mix until completely absorbed and no longer visible. Add remaining stock and greens; bring to a boil, reduce heat, and cook until greens and meat are tender, about 20 minutes. Serve over creamy grits, rice, or with boiled new potatoes. Additional broth would make it a great soup. However served, it needs a good, crusty bread. This is a sopping dish.

Marinated Pork Tenderloin with Sticky Rice and Mangoes

SERVES 4

1 pork tenderloin (1 to 2 pounds)
6 ounces Paula Deen Savannah
   Marinade
1¾ cups water
1 cup uncooked jasmine rice
1 can coconut milk
⅔ cup sugar

½ teaspoon salt
2 tablespoons olive oil
2 fresh mangoes, peeled and sliced
Toasted coconut, for garnish
   (optional)
Fresh flat-leaf parsley, for garnish
   (optional)

Place pork tenderloin and marinade in ziplock plastic bag. Massage marinade into tenderloin. Seal bag and place in refrigerator for 6 hours or overnight. Preheat oven to 350 degrees. In a medium saucepan, bring water to a boil. Add rice, stirring just to mix. Cover pan with tight-fitting lid, reduce heat to low, and simmer until water has been absorbed, about 20 to 25 minutes. In a small saucepan, combine coconut milk, sugar, and salt. Bring to a boil for 4 minutes, stirring constantly. Remove from heat and pour into cooked rice. Stir well. Place foil or waxed paper directly on rice mixture and let rest at room temperature for 30 minutes. While rice is resting, prepare tenderloin. Remove tenderloin from plastic bag and place on foil-lined baking sheet. Brush with olive oil and place in oven. Roast for 20 minutes per pound, or until internal temperature reaches 150 degrees. Remove from oven and let rest 10 minutes before slicing. To serve, place a scoop of sticky rice in the middle of a plate and top with sliced tenderloin. Top with sliced mangoes and garnish with toasted coconut and sprig of parsley, if desired.

The Lady's Oven-Roasted Ribs

SERVES 6

One 5-pound slab pork ribs
4 teaspoons liquid smoke
    (available in a bottle at
    grocery store)

2 teaspoons House Seasoning
    (see page 180)
2 teaspoons seasoned salt

Preheat oven to 325 degrees. Wash ribs and drain. Rub each side with liquid smoke, garlic powder, salt, pepper, and seasoned salt. Refrigerate for 4 to 24 hours. Roast uncovered for 1½ hours.

❦ ❦ ❦ **The Lady & Sons**

Sausage and Grits

SERVES 10

1 cup uncooked grits
1 pound ground sausage
1 onion, chopped
Two 4½-ounce cans green chilies,
    chopped
8 tablespoons (1 stick) butter

2 eggs, beaten
2 cups grated Cheddar cheese
10 dashes Tabasco
1 teaspoon paprika
¼ cup chopped fresh parsley

Preheat oven to 325 degrees. Cook grits in 4 cups salted water until thick. Sauté sausage, breaking it into small pieces. Sauté onion in sausage fat; drain. Add onion and chilies to sausage. Add butter, eggs, cheese, and Tabasco to grits. Combine grits mixture with sausage mixture. Pour into a 13 × 9-inch casserole dish and garnish with additional small amounts of cheese, chilies, paprika, and parsley. Bake for 1 hour. Can be refrigerated up to 2 days before baking. Freezes well.

Piggy Pudding

SERVES 4 TO 5

This is a great no-fuss recipe—wonderful for a brunch or Sunday-night supper.

16 link pork sausages
4 to 5 tart apples, peeled, cored,
   and sliced

One 7 ½-ounce package corn bread
   mix (prepare batter according
   to directions on package)

Preheat oven to 450 degrees. Cook sausages until done, piercing with fork to let out fat. Drain, then arrange in a 9-inch square baking dish. Layer sliced apples on top. Pour corn bread batter over all and bake for approximately 30 minutes or until corn bread is done. Serve with warm maple syrup.

Southern Fried Chicken

SERVES 4

My Grandmother Paul always said to season chicken and return it to the refrigerator and let it sit as long as time permits, at least 2 to 3 hours. At the restaurant, we season ours with House Seasoning and Lawry's Seasoned Salt. Always use small chickens. I find that a Dutch oven works best for frying chicken.

3 eggs
⅓ cup water
2 cups self-rising flour
1 teaspoon pepper

One 1- to 2½-pound chicken, cut
   into pieces
Crisco shortening for frying

Beat eggs with water. To just enough self-rising flour to coat all the chicken, add black pepper. Dip seasoned chicken in egg; coat well in flour mixture. Fry in moderately hot shortening (350°) until brown and crisp. Remember that dark meat requires longer cooking time (about 13 to 14 minutes, compared to 8 to 10 minutes for white meat).

❦ ❦ ❦ *The Lady & Sons*

Creole Burgers with Bayou Mayo

SERVES 8

*1 medium Vidalia onion, finely
  chopped*
2 cloves garlic, minced
1 red bell pepper, finely chopped
2 pounds ground chicken
1 egg

½ cup bread crumbs
2 teaspoons Creole seasoning
Salt and black pepper to taste
Bayou Mayo (see recipe below)
8 hamburger buns

Lightly spray a sauté pan with nonstick cooking spray. In the prepared pan, sauté onion, garlic, and bell pepper until tender. Set aside and allow to cool completely. In a large bowl, combine chicken and the cooled mixture. Add egg, bread crumbs, and Creole seasoning. Mix together well and form into 8 patties. Season each patty with salt and black pepper. Spray a large skillet with nonstick cooking spray and cook burgers until done, about 5 minutes on each side. While burgers are cooking, prepare Bayou Mayo.

BAYOU MAYO

YIELDS 1 CUP

1 cup mayonnaise
1 teaspoon Creole seasoning

Juice of 1 lemon
1 tablespoon chives, finely chopped

In a small mixing bowl, combine all ingredients.

To assemble burger, place patty on bottom bun half and top with generous dollop of Bayou Mayo. Cover with top bun and serve.

Chicken Pot Pie

SERVES 6 TO 8

One 10¾-ounce can condensed
 Cheddar cheese soup
One 10¾-ounce can condensed
 cream of celery soup
½ cup milk
1 chicken, skinned, cooked, boned,
 and cubed
1 medium onion, diced
One 10-ounce package frozen
 green peas (or one 8-ounce can,
 drained)

3 carrots, sliced, cooked, and
 drained
Salt and pepper to taste
1 pastry for top and bottom
 (see recipe below)
Butter to dot pastry

In a large saucepan, heat soups and milk. Stir in chicken, onion, peas, carrots, and salt and pepper. Cook until mixture boils. Remove from heat. Preheat oven to 350 degrees. Pour into a pastry-lined 13 × 9 × 2-inch pan. Cut pastry for top into strips. Lay over pie filling in a lattice style. Dot with butter. Bake for 45 minutes until golden brown.

PASTRY

3 cups all-purpose flour
1 teaspoon salt
¼ teaspoon baking powder

¾ cup Crisco shortening
Ice water

Sift together flour, salt, and baking powder. Cut in shortening with pastry blender until pieces are the size of small peas. Sprinkle 1 to 2 tablespoons of ice water over part of mixture. Gently toss with fork; push to side of bowl. Repeat until all is moistened. Form into 2 balls. Flatten each on a lightly floured surface by pressing with edge of hand three times across in both directions. With a floured rolling pin, roll out on floured surface. Roll from center to edge until ⅛ inch thick.

❀ ❀ ❀ **The Lady & Sons**

Chicken Brunswick Stew

SERVES 6 TO 8

One 2½-pound fryer
One 28-ounce can crushed tomatoes, sweetened with ⅓ cup sugar
One 16-ounce can creamed corn
1 cup ketchup
½ cup prepared barbecue sauce
1 tablespoon liquid smoke
  (available in a bottle at grocery
  store)

1 onion, chopped
1 tablespoon vinegar
1 tablespoon Worcestershire sauce
Salt and pepper to taste
Celery salt to taste

In a large pot, boil chicken until meat falls off bone, approximately 45 minutes; drain (reserve 1 to 2 cups of stock). Remove skin and bones; chop meat. In a separate pot, mix chicken and remaining ingredients. Simmer slowly for about 30 minutes, stirring often to prevent sticking. (Add a little bit of stock if stew gets too thick.) Serve over steamed rice.

🍀 🍀 🍀 **The Lady & Sons**

Pulled Barbecue Chicken Sandwich

SERVES 6

2 pounds skinless boneless chicken
  thighs
Kosher salt and freshly ground
  black pepper
2 tablespoons canola oil
1 onion, finely chopped
2 cloves garlic, finely chopped

3 tablespoons apple cider vinegar
1 cup ketchup
½ cup water
2 tablespoons light brown sugar
1 tablespoon Worcestershire sauce
¼ teaspoon cayenne pepper
6 whole-wheat hamburger buns

Season chicken thighs on both sides with salt and black pepper. Heat oil in a large high-sided skillet over medium-high heat. Once it shimmers, add chicken thighs and sear until golden brown, about 4 minutes on each side. Remove to a plate. Add onion and garlic and sauté until tender, about 3 minutes. Stir in apple cider vinegar, and using a wooden spoon, stir up any browned bits on the bottom of the pan. Add ketchup, water, brown sugar, Worcestershire sauce, cayenne pepper, and salt and black pepper to taste. Bring to a boil, then reduce heat to a simmer. Add chicken back to the pan, as well as juices that have accumulated on the plate. Simmer for 40 minutes. When chicken is cooked, shred meat with a fork in the skillet. Toss meat through the sauce so that it's covered. Divide pulled meat between 6 hamburger buns. Serve alongside coleslaw, if desired.

Baked Hen and Dressing

SERVES 8 TO 10

One 6-pound hen	1 tablespoon whole peppercorns
4 to 6 ribs celery, cut into large pieces	4 bay leaves
	1 large onion, peeled and left whole
2 tablespoons salt	3 chicken bouillon cubes

Remove giblets from bird. Wash giblets and bird well, inside and out. Place all ingredients including giblets in large pot, cover with water, and bring to a boil. Reduce heat and simmer until tender, approximately 2 to 2½ hours. Skim fat from pot at end of cooking time. (You will need to reserve stock for stuffing and gravy.) In the meantime, prepare and cook corn bread.

CORN BREAD

1 cup self-rising cornmeal	2 eggs
½ cup self-rising flour	2 tablespoons vegetable oil
¾ cup buttermilk	

Preheat oven to 350 degrees. Combine all ingredients and pour into a greased shallow baking dish. Bake for approximately 20 to 25 minutes. Remove from oven and let cool.

SOUTHERN CORN BREAD STUFFING

7 slices white bread (dried in warm oven)
Corn bread
1 sleeve saltine crackers
2 cups chopped celery
1 large onion, chopped
8 tablespoons (1 stick) butter
7 cups stock reserved from cooking hen

1 teaspoon salt
½ teaspoon pepper
1 teaspoon sage (optional)
1 tablespoon poultry seasoning (optional)
5 eggs, beaten

Preheat oven to 350 degrees. Crumble dried white bread slices, cornbread, and saltines; mix together and set aside. Sauté chopped celery and onion in butter until transparent, approximately 5 to 10 minutes. Pour over corn bread mixture. Add stock; mix well and taste; add salt, pepper, sage, and poultry seasoning. Add beaten eggs and mix well. Reserve 2 heaping tablespoons of this mixture for the giblet gravy. Pour into a greased pan. Place bird on top of dressing and bake until dressing is done, about 45 minutes. If hen browns too quickly, make a tent of foil and place over bird.

GIBLET GRAVY

4 cups stock reserved from cooking hen
Giblets from hen (liver, gizzard, and neck), chopped
2 chicken bouillon cubes
2 heaping tablespoons reserved uncooked corn bread stuffing mix

3 tablespoons cornstarch
⅓ cup cold water
1 hard-boiled egg, sliced
Salt and pepper to taste

Bring stock to a boil along with giblets and the meat that has been removed from the neck. Add bouillon cubes and raw stuffing mixture. Mix cornstarch with water and add to boiling stock, stirring constantly. Reduce heat and continue to cook for 2 to 3 minutes. Add salt and pepper to taste, and add sliced boiled egg. Serve with hen.

❧ ❧ ❧ *The Lady & Sons*

Chicken in Wine Sauce

SERVES 4

*4 large skinless boneless chicken
   breasts*
6 ounces Swiss cheese slices
*One 10¾-ounce can condensed
   cream of chicken soup*
¼ cup white wine (more if desired)

Salt and pepper to taste
*1 cup herb-flavored Pepperidge
   Farm stuffing mix, crushed*
*4 tablespoons (½ stick) butter,
   melted*

Preheat oven to 350 degrees. Place chicken in shallow buttered casserole. Layer cheese on top. Mix soup, wine, salt, and pepper; pour over cheese. Sprinkle stuffing mix on top and drizzle with melted butter. Bake for 45–60 minutes.

Roasted Turkey

SERVES 12

1½ teaspoons kosher salt
*½ teaspoon, plus ⅛ teaspoon black
   pepper*
*1 turkey (12 to 14 pounds),
   thawed if frozen*
1 onion, quartered
1 head of garlic, halved crosswise

*Several sprigs fresh herbs, such as
   thyme, parsley, rosemary, and sage*
2 bay leaves
½ cup unsalted butter, melted
One 14½-ounce can chicken broth
2 teaspoons chopped fresh thyme
¼ cup cornstarch

Preheat oven to 325 degrees. Sprinkle ½ teaspoon of the salt and ¼ teaspoon of the pepper inside turkey cavity. Place onion, garlic, herb sprigs, and bay leaves inside cavity. In a large roasting pan, place turkey on a rack, breast side up. Brush with half the butter; sprinkle with ¼ teaspoon pepper and remaining salt. Truss, if desired. Tent turkey with foil, roast for 2 hours and 30 minutes. Remove foil and brush with remaining butter. Increase oven temperature to 425 degrees. Roast turkey for about 45 minutes, until meat thermometer inserted into thickest part of thigh away from bone registers 180 degrees. Tent with foil during last 15 minutes of cooking time if browning too quickly.

Let stand 15 minutes before carving. Meanwhile, skim and discard fat from pan juices. Place roasting pan with 1½ cups pan juice over medium heat. Add broth, chopped thyme, and remaining pepper, stirring up browned bits from the bottom of the pan. Simmer for 3 minutes. Stir together cornstarch and ⅓ cup water. Strain gravy into small pot over low heat and gradually whisk in cornstarch mixture. Simmer, stirring, until thick, for about 2 minutes.

Chicken Paprika

SERVES 6 TO 8

1 large onion, chopped
1 clove garlic, minced
4 tablespoons olive oil
One 4- to 5-pound chicken, cut up
2 tablespoons paprika
1 teaspoon pepper

2 teaspoons salt
1½ cups water
1 cup sour cream
1 tablespoon all-purpose flour
Dumplings (optional)

In a deep skillet over medium heat, brown onion and garlic in oil. Add chicken and brown on all sides, about 10 minutes. Sprinkle paprika, pepper, and salt on chicken. Turn meat once. Add water, cover, and simmer on low heat for approximately 30 minutes or until meat is tender. Remove from liquid. In a small bowl, mix sour cream, flour, and 1 cup of hot liquid from chicken until smooth. Pour mixture into skillet and blend with remaining liquid. Add dumplings if desired and heat through. This dish may be served over noodles or rice instead of dumplings.

DUMPLINGS

3 eggs, beaten
3 cups all-purpose flour

1 teaspoon salt
½ cup water

Blend all ingredients and mix well. Drop batter by teaspoonfuls into boiling water. Cook about 10 minutes and drain. Rinse with cold water and drain again.

Chicken Georgia

SERVES 4 TO 6

4 tablespoons (½ stick) butter	2 tablespoons minced shallots
4 skinless boneless chicken breast halves	¼ teaspoon salt
	¼ teaspoon pepper
1 cup sliced fresh mushrooms	4 ounces grated mozzarella cheese

Melt butter over medium heat. Add mushrooms and shallots and sprinkle with salt and pepper. Cook 10 minutes. Add chicken and cook 10 minutes on each side, or until tender. Transfer chicken to platter and sprinkle with grated cheese. Top with mushroom mixture. Cover and let stand 5 minutes or until cheese melts.

Herbed Stuffed Chicken Breasts

SERVES 4

4 whole skinless boneless chicken breasts (approximately 5 to 7 ounces each)	½ teaspoon dried oregano
	½ teaspoon House Seasoning (see page 180)
One 3-ounce package cream cheese, softened	4 slices bacon
	1 leek (optional)
3 ounces feta cheese, crumbled	4 tablespoons (½ stick) butter, melted
½ teaspoon dried sweet basil	

Preheat oven to 275 degrees. Wash and pound each chicken breast flat. Lay chicken breast on cookie sheet or large platter and spread it with cream cheese, followed by a quarter of the feta cheese. Mix together basil, oregano, and House Seasoning and sprinkle over chicken. Roll up each breast and wrap with a slice of bacon. At this time, if desired, you can tie up each rolled chicken breast with the green top of a leek. Cut the green top off the vegetable, leaving it long enough to tie around the breast and allowing a couple of extra inches for a knot. Place chicken breasts in a casserole dish and pour melted butter over all. Cover casserole dish with foil and bake for 1½ hours. Uncover dish and increase temperature to 350 degrees. Continue to bake, allowing the bacon to brown, for 15 to 20 minutes. Or you could place dish under broiler for a few minutes to brown. Serve over rice, with pan juices poured on top.

Paula's Chicken and Waffles

SERVES 4

Peanut oil for frying
1½ pounds skinless boneless chicken
    tenders
Kosher salt and freshly ground
    black pepper
1 cup all-purpose flour
2 teaspoons garlic powder

1 cup buttermilk
1 cup panko bread crumbs
One 24-ounce package Paula Deen
    Original Recipes Biscuit Mix
Maple syrup, for serving
The Lady & Sons Signature Hot
    Sauce, for serving

In a deep fryer or Dutch oven, heat oil to 350 degrees. Season chicken tenders on both sides with salt and pepper. In a medium casserole dish, whisk together flour and garlic powder. Place buttermilk in a second casserole dish. Place bread crumbs in a third casserole dish. Dredge seasoned tenders through flour, buttermilk, and bread crumbs. Add chicken to deep fryer and fry for 4 minutes, until golden brown and crisp and an instant-read thermometer reads 165 degrees. Drain on a paper towel–lined plate. Prepare waffle batter as directed on package. Cook waffles according to directions for your waffle iron. Usually it will take 4 to 6 minutes for waffles to turn golden and the waffle iron to stop releasing steam, which indicates that they're done. Serve waffles topped with fried chicken. Serve with maple syrup or hot sauce.

Honey Game Hens

SERVES 6

6 Cornish game hens (about ¾ to
   1 pound each)
4 cloves garlic, chopped
One 1-inch piece of ginger, peeled
   and chopped

½ cup soy sauce
½ cup honey
2 tablespoons peanut oil
2 tablespoons orange juice
1 tablespoon orange zest, minced

Rinse hens, trim off excess fat, and pat dry; place in bowl. Put garlic and ginger in food processor and process until nearly smooth. In another bowl, combine soy sauce, honey, oil, orange juice, and zest. Add the garlic and ginger. Pour mixture over game hens, coating well. Refrigerate overnight, turning in marinade several times. Preheat oven to 350 degrees. Place game hens in shallow roasting pan; pour marinade on top. Bake for 1 hour, basting every 15 minutes. Remove hens to serving platter. Pour cooking juices into small, heavy saucepan and boil for 5 minutes, or until sauce thickens. Pour over hens just before serving. Serve with sesame noodles or rice pilaf. These hens can also be grilled—just remember to baste often.

Pecan Chicken

SERVES 8

8 tablespoons (1 stick) butter
1 cup buttermilk
1 egg, lightly beaten
1 cup all-purpose flour
1 cup ground pecans
1 tablespoon salt

1 tablespoon paprika
⅛ teaspoon pepper
¼ cup sesame seeds
Two 2½-pound chickens, cut into
   quarters or pieces
¼ cup pecan halves

Preheat oven to 350 degrees. Melt butter in a 10 × 15-inch baking pan. In a shallow dish, combine buttermilk and egg. In another dish combine flour, pecans, salt, paprika, pepper, and sesame seeds. Dip chicken in buttermilk, then in flour. Place skin side down in melted butter. Turn to coat and leave skin side up. Sprinkle with pecan halves. Bake for 1¼ hours.

Stuffed Turkey Breast

SERVES 6 TO 8

2 tablespoons canola oil

1 medium onion, diced

1 stalk celery, diced

2 tablespoons butter

2 cloves garlic, minced

1 tablespoon chopped fresh sage, plus
 sprig for garnish

1 tablespoon chopped fresh thyme,
 plus sprig for garnish

2 cups cubed and dried corn bread

½ cup chopped pecans, toasted

⅓ cup dried cranberries

½ cup chicken broth

Kosher salt and freshly ground
 black pepper

1 boneless turkey breast, about
 3 pounds

Preheat oven to 400 degrees. Heat canola oil in a large skillet over medium heat. Once hot, add onion and celery and sauté until soft and translucent. Add butter and garlic and cook for 2 minutes more, until fragrant. Add sage, thyme, corn bread, pecans, cranberries, and chicken broth, stirring well with a wooden spoon to fully incorporate. Let flavors marry and warm on stove top for 2 to 3 minutes. Season stuffing with salt and black pepper. Remove from heat and let cool slightly. Carefully remove skin from turkey breast, being careful not to tear it. Place turkey breast, skin side up, on a cutting board. Holding a knife parallel to the work surface, slice through the breast, almost in half, without cutting all the way through. Open the breast like a book. Lay turkey between two sheets of plastic wrap and, using a meat mallet, pound out to an even thickness, about ½ to ¾ inch. Remove turkey from plastic wrap, season with salt and pepper. Spread stuffing evenly across turkey breast, leaving a ¾-inch border all around the edges. Roll turkey breast over stuffing, creating a uniform log. Do not roll too tight or stuffing will fall out. Wrap skin around the breast, hiding the seam of the log. Use kitchen twine to tie and secure the shape, while keeping stuffing intact. Season outside of turkey with salt and pepper. Roast until a thermometer inserted into stuffing registers 155 degrees, about 45 minutes. Remove from oven and let rest, tented with foil, for 15 minutes. The temperature should reach 165 after resting. Trim kitchen twine and slice. Garnish with fresh herbs.

Chicken and Rice Casserole

SERVES 6 TO 8

3 cups diced cooked chicken
1 medium onion, diced and
   sautéed
One 8-ounce can water chestnuts,
   drained and chopped
Two 14½-ounce cans French green
   beans, rinsed and drained
One 4-ounce can pimentos, rinsed
   and drained

One 10¾-ounce can condensed
   cream of celery soup
1 cup mayonnaise
One 6-ounce box Uncle Ben's long-
   grain and wild rice, cooked
   according to package directions
1 cup grated sharp Cheddar cheese

Preheat oven to 300 degrees. Mix all ingredients together and pour into a 3-quart casserole. Bake for 25 minutes.

❧ ❧ ❧ *The Lady & Sons*

Chicken and Dumplings

SERVES 4 TO 6

One 2½-pound chicken
3 ribs celery, chopped
1 large onion, chopped
2 bay leaves
2 chicken bouillon cubes
1 teaspoon House Seasoning
   (see page 180)

4 quarts water
One 10¾-ounce can condensed
   cream of celery or cream of
   chicken soup

Cut up chicken, but do not remove skin. The skin and bones can be removed later. Place chicken, celery, onion, bay leaves, bouillon, and House Seasoning in water and boil at a rolling boil for 30 to 45 minutes, until meat begins to fall off the bones. Remove skin and bones at this point, along with bay leaves. Return chicken to pan. Prepare dumplings and set them aside for a few minutes. Add cream soup to chicken and continue to boil. If desired, you can thicken the stock a little by mixing 2 tablespoons cornstarch with ¼ cup of water and adding it to the stock. Drop dumplings into boiling stock. Never stir dumplings. Shake the pot gently in a circular motion to submerge dumplings in stock. Cook for a few minutes more, until dumplings are done. Do not overcook.

DUMPLINGS

2 cups all-purpose flour mixed   *¾ cup ice water*
with 1 teaspoon salt

Put flour in a mixing bowl. Beginning in center of flour, dribble small amount of ice water. Work mixture with fingers from center of bowl to sides of bowl, incorporating small amounts of water at a time. Continue until all flour is used up. Batter will feel as if it is going to be tough. Knead dough and form into ball. Dust a good amount of flour onto dough board and rolling pin. Roll out dough, working from center. Dough will be firm. Roll to ⅛ inch thinness. Let it air-dry for a minute or two while you return your attention to the boiling pot at the point at which you add the canned soup to the chicken mixture. Cut dumplings into 1-inch strips. Working with one strip at a time, hold strip over pot, pull it in half, and drop into the boiling stock. Remember, do not stir mixture after dumplings have been added to pot.

❦ ❦ ❦ *The Lady & Sons*

NOTE: Frozen dumplings are available in most supermarkets if you don't have the time to make them.

Buffalo Chicken Livers
with Blue Cheese Dipping Sauce

SERVES 4

½ pound (2 sticks) butter
½ cup The Lady & Sons Signature
   Hot Sauce
Peanut oil for deep-frying
   (or canola or vegetable oil)
1 cup all-purpose flour
1 teaspoon salt
½ teaspoon paprika

½ teaspoon garlic powder
½ teaspoon cayenne pepper
¼ teaspoon black pepper
1 pound chicken livers, soaked in
   milk
1 cup blue cheese dressing
4 ounces blue cheese, crumbled

To make buffalo sauce, in a small saucepan, heat butter and hot sauce just until butter melts; keep warm until ready to use. In a deep fryer or Dutch oven, heat oil to 375 degrees. In a ziplock bag, combine flour, salt, paprika, garlic powder, cayenne pepper, and black pepper. Add chicken livers to ziplock bag and shake gently until coated. Deep-fry livers, 8 to 10 pieces at a time, for 10 to 12 minutes, turning once or twice. Drain livers on paper towel–lined baking sheet for 30 seconds. Transfer buffalo sauce to a large mixing bowl; in batches, immediately toss fried livers in buffalo sauce and remove with a slotted spoon. To make dipping sauce, in a small bowl, stir together blue cheese dressing and crumbled blue cheese.

Herb-Baked Chicken

SERVES 4

One 1- to 2-pound chicken, cut in
   quarters, skin removed
3 to 4 tablespoons olive oil
¼ cup teriyaki sauce
¼ teaspoon dried oregano

¼ teaspoon dried rosemary
1 teaspoon chopped fresh ginger
½ teaspoon salt
⅛ teaspoon pepper
1 lemon, sliced thin

Preheat oven to 350 degrees. Coat chicken with oil and place in baking dish. Sprinkle with teriyaki sauce. Combine oregano, rosemary, ginger, salt, and pepper; sprinkle over chicken. Top with lemon slices. Bake for about 1 hour.

Marinated Cornish Hens

SERVES 2 TO 4

2 split Cornish hens
1 onion, diced
1 clove garlic, minced
8 tablespoons (1 stick) butter
One 10¾-ounce can beef broth

1 bay leaf
¼ teaspoon dried thyme
2 tablespoons sherry
Salt and pepper to taste
16 ounces fresh mushrooms, sliced

Wash, pat dry, and salt and pepper hens. Place in long, flat baking dish. Sauté onion and garlic in butter. Add remaining ingredients except the mushrooms. Stir and pour over hens; cover and refrigerate overnight. Preheat oven to 350 degrees. Add mushrooms and bake for 1 hour, basting frequently. Serve with wild rice.

VARIATION: Chicken can be substituted for Cornish hens.

Chicken Casserole

SERVES 6 TO 8

1 fryer, cooked, boned, and cut
   into small pieces (reserve broth)
½ cup mayonnaise
½ cup chopped onion
4 eggs
8 tablespoons (1 stick) butter,
   melted

2½ cups chicken broth
1 package Pepperidge Farm corn
   bread stuffing mix
1 cup milk
One 10¾-ounce can condensed
   cream of chicken soup

Combine chicken, mayonnaise, and chopped onion and set aside. Combine 2 eggs, the butter, chicken broth, and corn bread stuffing mix and set aside. In small bowl, lightly beat 2 eggs and milk. Spray large casserole dish with nonstick cooking spray. In bottom of dish, spread half the stuffing mixture; then layer with chicken mixture. Add second layer of stuffing mixture. Pour egg and milk mixture over top layer of stuffing mixture. Refrigerate overnight. Preheat oven to 350 degrees. Spread cream of chicken soup on top of casserole and bake for 45 minutes.

Chicken Breasts in Sour Cream Sauce

SERVES 6 TO 8

8 slices dried beef (in a jar)
8 skinless boneless chicken breast
halves (7 ounces each)
4 slices bacon, cut in half

1 cup sour cream
One 10¾-ounce can condensed
cream of mushroom soup
2 cups sliced fresh mushrooms

Preheat oven to 300 degrees. Lay one piece of dried beef on each chicken breast and wrap with a half slice of bacon. Place in a 13 × 9-inch casserole dish, seam side down. Mix sour cream, soup, and mushrooms together. Pour over chicken breasts. Cover and bake for 1½ hours. Serve with rice.

Duck Burgundy

SERVES 4 TO 6

The flavor in this recipe really comes out if you can let the duck marinate in the seasoning for a few hours or overnight.

4 whole ducks
Salt and pepper to taste
Garlic powder to taste
Poultry seasoning to taste
1 large onion, quartered
1 apple, quartered

1 orange, quartered
4 ribs celery, cut into 1-inch pieces
⅓ cup soy sauce
⅓ cup vegetable oil
½ cup red Burgundy wine

Preheat oven to 450 degrees. Clean ducks well and rub body cavities lightly with salt, pepper, garlic powder, and poultry seasoning. Stuff cavities with pieces of onion, apple, orange, and celery. Rub ducks with soy sauce and oil. Place in baking pan. Roast uncovered, basting often with Burgundy wine. Allow 10 to 15 minutes baking time per pound of duck. Remove stuffing before serving.

Vegetables and Side Dishes

Cheesy Broccoli Bake

2 pounds fresh broccoli, trimmed
   and cut up
¼ cup chopped celery
¼ pound fresh mushrooms, sliced
¼ cup chopped onion
2 tablespoons butter
One 8-ounce can sliced water
   chestnuts

One 10¾-ounce can condensed
   cream of mushroom soup
½ pound Velveeta
½ teaspoon garlic salt
¼ teaspoon pepper
1 cup grated Cheddar cheese

Preheat oven to 350 degrees. Steam broccoli for 10 minutes. Sauté celery, mushrooms, and onion in butter for 10 minutes; drain. Combine broccoli, sauté mixture, and water chestnuts. Heat soup and Velveeta in saucepan over low heat until cheese melts. Pour over broccoli mixture. Stir in garlic salt and pepper. Place in greased casserole dish. Bake for 25 minutes. Sprinkle top with grated Cheddar.

Baked Grits

SERVES 6

4 cups water
1½ teaspoons salt
1 cup uncooked grits
2 eggs, beaten
8 tablespoons (1 stick) butter

1½ cups grated Monterey Jack and
   Cheddar cheese (combined)
2 cloves garlic, crushed
Dash of cayenne pepper

Preheat oven to 350 degrees. Bring water and salt to a boil. Add grits to boiling water, stirring constantly for a minute. Cover and cook, stirring occasionally, until grits are thick and creamy. Temper eggs with a small amount of hot cooked grits, then add back to remaining grits. Combine remaining ingredients with grits and pour into a 2-quart casserole dish. Bake for 45 minutes. Top with additional cheese, if desired. ❦ ❦ ❦ *The Lady & Sons*

Squash Casserole

SERVES 6

1 large onion, chopped
4 tablespoons (½ stick) butter
3 cups cooked squash, drained,
   with all water squeezed out
1 cup crushed Ritz crackers, plus
   additional for topping

½ cup sour cream
1 teaspoon House Seasoning
   (see page 180)
1 cup grated Cheddar cheese

Preheat oven to 350 degrees. Sauté onion in butter for 5 minutes. Remove from pan and mix all ingredients together. Pour into buttered casserole dish and top with cracker crumbs. Bake for 25 to 30 minutes.

❦ ❦ ❦ **The Lady & Sons**

VARIATION: For a different taste in this casserole, layer slices of cooked red potatoes in the bottom of the casserole dish, followed by squash mixture; repeat layers. Top with about 1 cup Ritz crumbs tossed with melted butter.

Sherry-Glazed Sweet Potatoes

SERVES 6

3 large sweet potatoes or yams
6 slices canned pineapple
4 tablespoons (½ stick) butter

½ cup brown sugar
½ cup sherry

Preheat oven to 375 degrees. Boil potatoes, with skins on, for 20 to 30 minutes, or until tender. Drain and allow to cool. Peel and cut lengthwise into halves. Arrange slices of pineapple in a single layer in a greased shallow baking dish; place a potato half (cut side down) on top of each pineapple slice. Heat butter, brown sugar, and sherry together until sugar is dissolved; pour over potatoes and pineapple. Bake for 30 minutes, basting often with syrup in dish.

Turnip Greens with Cornmeal Dumplings

SERVES 4 TO 6

¾ *pound smoked meat (smoked*
turkey wings are excellent)
4 *quarts water*
1 *teaspoon House Seasoning*
(see page 180)
2 *chicken bouillon cubes*

¼ *teaspoon ground ginger*
1 *bunch turnip greens with roots*
4 *tablespoons (½ stick) butter*
1 *teaspoon sugar (optional; may be*
used if greens are bitter)

Place smoked meat in water along with House Seasoning, bouillon, and ginger. Cook over low heat for 1½ hours. Strip turnip leaves free of the big stem that runs down the center of each leaf. Wash in a sink full of clean water. Drain and wash twice more, since greens can often be sandy. Peel and slice or quarter roots. Add greens to meat; cook for another 30 minutes, stirring often. Add roots and continue to cook for approximately 15 minutes or until roots are tender. (Reserve ⅔ cup liquid after cooking if making dumplings.) Add butter and dumplings (if desired) and serve.

CORNMEAL DUMPLINGS

1 *cup all-purpose cornmeal*
½ *teaspoon salt*
1 *small onion, chopped*

1 *egg*
⅔ *cup liquid from cooked turnips*

Mix all ingredients together. Dipping by teaspoonfuls, gently roll batter in the palms of your hands into approximately 1-inch balls; drop into boiling turnip liquid. Make sure each dumpling is completely covered in liquid by shaking the pot gently; do not stir. Boil for about 10 minutes.

Steakside Mushrooms

SERVES 8

1½ pounds fresh mushrooms, sliced
    lengthwise
8 tablespoons (1 stick) butter

Jane's Krazy Mixed-Up Salt
¼ cup Worcestershire sauce
¼ cup water

In large skillet, sauté sliced mushrooms in butter until brown. Sprinkle liberally with Krazy salt. Add Worcestershire sauce and simmer until almost all sauce is absorbed by mushrooms. Add water and continue to simmer until mushrooms are tender. Great with steak or roast beef.

The Lady's Cheesy Mac

SERVES 6 TO 8

4 cups cooked elbow macaroni,
    drained (approximately 2 cups
    uncooked)
2 cups grated Cheddar cheese
3 eggs, beaten
½ cup sour cream

4 tablespoons (½ stick) butter, cut
    into pieces
½ teaspoon salt
1 cup milk, or equivalent in
    evaporated milk

Preheat oven to 350 degrees. After macaroni has been boiled and drained, add Cheddar cheese while macaroni is still hot. Combine remaining ingredients and add to macaroni mixture. Pour into casserole dish and bake for 30 to 45 minutes. Top with additional cheese, if desired.

Twice-Baked Potatoes

SERVES 6

This recipe can be frozen and whipped out whenever company comes over. Also try stuffing the potatoes with different kinds of cheese, sautéed shrimp, etc. Makes a great meal with a green salad.

6 large Idaho potatoes (as large and oval as possible)
Vegetable oil to coat
8 tablespoons (1 stick) butter

2 cups sour cream
Salt and pepper to taste
1 teaspoon dried parsley
Paprika

Preheat oven to 350 degrees. Wash potatoes, pat dry, prick sides gently with fork, and coat each potato entirely with oil. Place on foil-covered pan. Bake for at least 1 hour. In large bowl, place 1 stick of butter. Remove potatoes from oven and slice off top third of each one. Gently scoop out potato with spoon (potato skins should be crisp) and place into bowl. With mixer on high, mix potatoes, butter, sour cream, salt, and pepper. Add parsley and continue mixing until smooth. Gently stuff mixture back into potato shells, being careful not to break them. Pile potato mixture as high as you can above top of potato shell. Sprinkle with paprika for color. (Can be frozen at this point for serving later.) Bake again for about 20 to 30 minutes. Should be lightly browned on top.

Savannah Red Rice

SERVES 4 TO 6

1 cup chopped onion
1 cup chopped bell pepper
2 tablespoons butter
1 cup diced Hillshire Farms sausage
One 14½-ounce can crushed
    tomatoes with juice
1 tablespoon Texas Pete or red hot
    sauce

1 cup tomato sauce
1 cup water
3 chicken bouillon cubes
Pepper to taste; add salt to taste if
    desired
1 cup uncooked white rice

Preheat oven to 350 degrees. In a saucepan over medium heat, sauté onion and bell pepper in butter. Add sausage; heat until mixture is slightly browned. Add tomatoes, hot sauce, tomato sauce, water, and bouillon cubes. Season with pepper and salt as needed. Stir in rice. Pour mixture into a greased casserole and bake for 45 minutes.

❦ ❦ ❦ **The Lady & Sons**

Mashed Cauliflower

SERVES 4

1 medium head cauliflower, cut
    into florets
⅓ cup chicken broth, warmed
2 tablespoons light sour cream

Salt and black pepper
Thinly sliced fresh chives,
    for garnish

Place cauliflower florets in a microwave-safe bowl with ¼ cup water, cover with plastic wrap, and microwave for 3 to 5 minutes, or until completely tender. Place cooked cauliflower in a food processor. Add chicken broth, sour cream, salt, and black pepper and puree until smooth. Serve garnished with sliced chives.

Collard Greens

SERVES 4 TO 6

½ pound smoked meat (ham hocks, smoked turkey wings, or smoked neck bones)
1 tablespoon House Seasoning (see page 180)

1 tablespoon seasoned salt
1 tablespoon Texas Pete hot sauce
1 large bunch of collards
8 tablespoons (1 stick) butter

In a large pot, bring 3 quarts of water to a boil and add smoked meat, House Seasoning, seasoned salt, and hot sauce. Reduce heat to medium and cook for 1 hour. In the meantime, wash collard greens thoroughly. Remove the thick stem that runs down the center of the greens by holding the leaf in your left hand and stripping the leaf down with your right hand (the tender young leaves in the heart of the collards don't need to be stripped). Stack 6 to 8 stripped leaves on top of each other, roll up, and slice into ½- to 1-inch-thick slices. Place greens in pot with cooked smoked meat. Add butter after greens. Cook for 45 to 60 minutes, stirring occasionally. When done, taste and adjust seasoning.

Eggplant Casserole

SERVES 4

1 large eggplant
1¾ cups crushed Ritz crackers
1½ cups grated American cheese
8 tablespoons (1 stick) butter, melted

2 eggs
⅔ cup milk
1 teaspoon House Seasoning (see page 180)

Preheat oven to 350 degrees. Peel, slice, and boil eggplant for 10 to 15 minutes, until tender; drain. Divide cracker crumbs, cheese, and butter in half. To eggplant, add eggs, milk, House Seasoning, and half the crumbs, cheese, and butter. Mix well; pour into baking dish. Top with remaining half of the crumbs, cheese, and butter. Bake for 20 to 30 minutes.   ❧ ❧ ❧ *The Lady & Sons*

Vidalia Onion Pie

SERVES 8

Vidalia onions are Georgia's most famous taste. This sweet onion is grown in southeast Georgia, just a few miles west of Savannah. They can be stored in a cool dry place to use throughout the year.

3 cups thinly sliced Vidalia onion
3 tablespoons butter, melted
One 9-inch prebaked deep-dish pie
   shell
½ cup milk
1½ cups sour cream

1 teaspoon salt
2 eggs, beaten
3 tablespoons all-purpose flour
4 slices bacon, crisply cooked and
   crumbled

Preheat oven to 325 degrees. Sauté onion in butter until lightly browned. Spoon into pie shell. Combine milk, sour cream, salt, eggs, and flour. Mix well and pour over onion mixture. Garnish with bacon. Bake for 30 minutes or until firm in center. Pie has taste and texture of a quiche. ❧ ❧ ❧ **The Lady & Sons**

Sweet Potato Chips

SERVES 4

2 large sweet potatoes
8 tablespoons (1 stick) butter,
   melted

1 cup honey-roasted peanuts,
   chopped
Salt to taste

Preheat oven to 450 degrees. Line two large baking sheets with foil; lightly grease. Slice potatoes to ¼ inch thick. Dip potatoes in melted butter and arrange on baking sheet so that chips do not overlap. Sprinkle with peanuts. Bake for 15 to 20 minutes. Sprinkle with salt.

Broccoli Soufflé

SERVES 10

Three 10-ounce packages frozen
  chopped broccoli
¾ cup chicken stock
¾ cup whipping cream
8 tablespoons (1 stick) butter
½ cup all-purpose flour

4 eggs, separated
2 teaspoons chopped fresh parsley
3 tablespoons minced onion
Salt and pepper to taste
½ cup grated Monterey Jack or
  Cheddar cheese

Preheat oven to 425 degrees. Cook and drain broccoli. Add stock to cream and scald. Melt butter and blend in flour. Gradually add to cream mixture. Stir over medium heat until thick. Remove from heat and beat in egg yolks, parsley, onion, salt, and pepper. Stir in broccoli and cheese. When ready to serve, add stiffly beaten egg whites and pour into a buttered casserole dish. Bake for 25 to 30 minutes.

Quick Collard Green Sauté

SERVES 4

1 large bunch collard greens
2 tablespoons olive oil
3 cloves garlic, minced
½ teaspoon red pepper flakes

Kosher salt and freshly ground
  black pepper to taste
¼ cup chicken broth

Wash collard greens thoroughly. Remove the stem that runs down the center of each leaf by holding the stem in your left hand and stripping the leaf down with your right hand. The tender young leaves in the heart of collards don't need to be stripped. Stack 6 to 8 leaves on top of one another, roll up, and cut into ½-inch-thick slices. Heat a large sauté pan over medium-high heat and add olive oil. Once hot, add garlic and red pepper flakes and sauté until fragrant. Add collard greens and sauté until bright green, about 4 minutes. Season with salt and pepper. Stir in chicken broth and cook until liquid evaporates, another 2 minutes.

Boursin Cheese Potatoes

SERVES 8

3 pounds red potatoes, unpeeled
Salt and pepper to taste
1 pint heavy cream

One 5-ounce package Boursin
   cheese
Fresh chives or parsley, chopped

Preheat oven to 350 degrees. Wash and slice potatoes into ¼-inch-thick rounds. Toss potatoes with salt and pepper. Heat cream and cheese together, on top of stove or in microwave, until cheese has melted. Stir mixture until thoroughly blended. Layer half of the potatoes into a 2-quart baking dish (this is best if done in a deep dish instead of a long, flat dish). Cover potatoes with half of the cream mixture. Repeat with remaining potatoes and cream mixture. Cover and bake for 1 hour. Sprinkle top with chopped chives or parsley.

Fried Green Tomatoes

SERVES 6

Quite frequently I walk the dining room with a plate piled high with this wonderful fried fruit. The guests seem to enjoy this extra treat. My grandmother always used cornmeal, but I prefer flour.

3 or 4 large, firm green tomatoes
Salt
2 cups self-rising flour or cornmeal

1 to 2 teaspoons pepper
Vegetable oil for frying

Slice tomatoes to desired thickness (I prefer mine thin). Lay out on a pan and sprinkle with salt. Place in a colander and allow time for salt to pull the water out of tomatoes. Mix flour with pepper. Coat tomatoes with flour mixture and deep-fry until golden brown.

❧ ❧ ❧ *The Lady & Sons*

Southern Baked Beans

SERVES 3 TO 4

½ pound bacon
1 large onion, diced
One 16-ounce can pork and beans
3 tablespoons yellow mustard

5 tablespoons maple or pancake
  syrup
4 tablespoons ketchup

Preheat oven to 325 degrees. Fry bacon until crisp; crumble. In bacon drippings, sauté onion until brown. Mix bacon, onion, and drippings with remaining ingredients. Pour into casserole dish and bake covered for 45 to 60 minutes. ❦ ❦ ❦ *The Lady & Sons*

Zucchini and Corn Casserole

SERVES 4 TO 5

1½ pounds small zucchini
One 8-ounce can cream-style corn
2 eggs, lightly beaten
1 small onion, chopped
1 small bell pepper, chopped

1 tablespoon butter
½ teaspoon salt
¼ teaspoon ground black pepper
½ cup grated sharp Cheddar cheese
Paprika to taste

Preheat oven to 350 degrees. Cook zucchini in boiling salted water to cover until just tender, about 6 minutes. Drain, cut into chunks, and combine with corn and eggs. Meanwhile, sauté onion and bell pepper in butter until golden brown, about 5 minutes. Add to zucchini and corn mixture; add salt and pepper. Pour mixture into a greased casserole. Sprinkle cheese on top, then sprinkle with paprika. Bake uncovered for about 30 minutes, or until lightly browned and bubbly.

Savory Rice

SERVES 4

1 cup chopped onion
8 tablespoons (1 stick) butter
One 10 ¾-ounce can beef broth
One 10 ¾-ounce can condensed
    French onion soup

One 4 ½-ounce can mushroom
    pieces, drained
1 cup uncooked white rice

Preheat oven to 350 degrees. In saucepan over medium heat, sauté onion in butter until almost tender. Remove from heat. Stir in broth, onion soup, mushrooms, and uncooked rice. Pour into casserole dish. Bake for about 1 hour, or until done.

Mashed Potatoes

SERVES 8

8 to 10 medium red new potatoes,
    skin on
½ cup hot milk

8 tablespoons (1 stick) butter
½ cup sour cream
Salt and pepper to taste

Slice potatoes ¼ inch thick. Cook in boiling water for 15 minutes or until fork-tender. Whip unpeeled cooked potatoes with electric mixer; mix until moderately smooth. Don't overbeat them; a few lumps are nice. Add hot milk, butter, and sour cream. Salt and pepper to taste. Whip until mixed. Adjust thickness by adding more milk, if desired.

❦ ❦ ❦ *The Lady & Sons*

Fresh Corn Scallop

SERVES 6

6 ears fresh corn
2 tablespoons all-purpose flour
1 teaspoon sugar
1¼ teaspoons salt

⅛ teaspoon pepper
½ cup milk
¾ cup buttered dry bread crumbs

Preheat oven to 375 degrees. Cut corn off cob, being careful not to cut too deep. This should make 2½ to 3 cups of corn. Combine corn, flour, sugar, salt, pepper, and milk. Sprinkle half the crumbs over bottom of 1-quart casserole dish. Add corn mixture. Bake covered for 30 minutes. Remove cover and sprinkle with remaining crumbs. Bake uncovered 20 minutes more.

Sweet Potato Bake

SERVES 8

3 cups peeled, cooked, and mashed
   sweet potatoes or yams
1 cup sugar
⅓ cup butter, melted
2 eggs

1 teaspoon vanilla
1 teaspoon ground cinnamon
¼ teaspoon ground nutmeg
¼ cup heavy cream, half-and-half,
   or whole milk

Preheat oven to 325 degrees. Mix all ingredients together except for cream. Beat with electric mixer until smooth. Add cream; mix well. Pour into greased casserole dish. Add topping. Bake for 25 to 30 minutes.

TOPPING

1 cup brown sugar
1 cup walnuts, chopped

⅓ cup all-purpose flour
3 tablespoons butter, melted

Mix together with fork; sprinkle over top of casserole.

Tomato Pie

SERVES 6

4 tomatoes, peeled and sliced
8 to 10 fresh basil leaves, chopped
⅓ cup chopped green onion
One 9-inch prebaked deep-dish pie
   shell

Salt and pepper to taste
2 cups grated mozzarella and
   Cheddar cheese (combined)
1 cup mayonnaise

Preheat oven to 350 degrees. Layer tomato slices, basil, and onion in
pie shell. Add salt and pepper to taste. Mix together grated cheese and
mayonnaise. Spread on top of tomatoes. Bake for 30 minutes or until
lightly browned.

Broccoli Casserole

SERVES 2 TO 3

One 10-ounce package frozen
   chopped broccoli
1 small onion, chopped
4 tablespoons (½ stick) butter
½ cup grated Cheddar cheese
½ cup crushed Ritz crackers

½ cup condensed cream of mushroom soup
¼ cup mayonnaise
House Seasoning (see page 180)
   to taste

Preheat oven to 350 degrees. Steam broccoli until limp, about 10
minutes. Remove from heat; drain. Sauté onion in butter and add to
broccoli. Add all remaining ingredients; mix well. Pour mixture into a
casserole dish. Add topping.

TOPPING

½ cup crushed Ritz crackers

1 tablespoon butter, melted

Combine crackers and melted butter for topping; sprinkle on top of
casserole. Bake for 20 to 25 minutes.   🍀 🍀 🍀 **The Lady & Sons**

Susan's Baked Rice

SERVES 4

1 large onion, chopped
1 large bell pepper, chopped
8 tablespoons (1 stick) butter
4 or 5 chicken bouillon cubes

1 cup uncooked white rice
2 cups water
Ground black pepper to taste

Preheat oven to 350 degrees. Sauté onion and bell pepper in butter; add bouillon cubes. Stir until dissolved. Combine rice and water and add to mixture. Pour into a 13 × 9-inch baking dish. Sprinkle with pepper. Bake for 45 minutes. Goes great with baked or fried chicken.

❦ ❦ ❦ *The Lady & Sons*

Potato Casserole

SERVES 6

Leftover mashed potatoes work wonderfully in this recipe.

2 cups mashed potatoes
½ cup sour cream
House Seasoning (see page 180)
   to taste
1 small onion, sliced thin

1 small bell pepper, sliced thin
8 tablespoons (1 stick) butter
1½ cups grated Cheddar cheese
4 medium potatoes, cooked
6 slices bacon, cooked crisp

Preheat oven to 350 degrees. Spread mashed potatoes evenly on bottom of casserole dish. Layer sour cream evenly over top. (Each time you add a layer, sprinkle on a little House Seasoning.) Sauté onion and bell pepper in butter; evenly layer over top of sour cream. Next, layer with ½ cup Cheddar cheese. Slice potatoes and layer over cheese until top is completely covered with potatoes. Finally, top with remaining 1 cup cheese. Bake for 25 to 30 minutes. Remove from oven and crumble bacon over top.

❦ ❦ ❦ *The Lady & Sons*

Creamed Corn

SERVES 3 TO 4

1 dozen ears fresh corn
8 tablespoons (1 stick) butter

Salt and pepper to taste

Remove corn from cob using a corn grater. (If you have to cut corn with a knife, avoid whole kernels; try mashing a little.) Put corn in glass dish and put stick of butter on top. Cook in microwave on high about 7 to 10 minutes, stopping to turn and stir a couple of times. Be careful not to overcook corn. If it seems too dry, add a little milk or water. Season with salt and pepper to taste. ❧ ❧ ❧ **The Lady & Sons**

Pattypan Summer Squash Casserole

SERVES 6

4 medium white pattypan summer
  squash
2 small onions, chopped
1 clove garlic, minced
4 tablespoons (½ stick) butter
2 slices white bread

1 medium bowl ice water
1 egg
Salt and pepper to taste
2 tablespoons chopped fresh parsley
1 cup cracker crumbs (or enough to
  cover casserole)

Preheat oven to 350 degrees. Peel and cut squash into cubes. Boil until tender, about 5 to 7 minutes, and drain. Brown onion and garlic in 2 tablespoons butter. Soak bread in ice water and wring out; chop fine. Add to onion and garlic; cook, stirring, for 2 to 3 minutes. Add drained squash and cook 2 to 3 minutes more, stirring. Beat egg and add, allowing it to absorb into the mixture. Cook 3 to 4 minutes. Season with salt and pepper and add parsley. Stir and remove from heat. Place in casserole dish or baking pan. Cover top with cracker crumbs and dot with remaining butter. Bake for 20 to 25 minutes, until the crumbs brown.

Hoppin' John

SERVES 6 TO 8

2 cups black-eyed peas, cooked
2 cups cooked rice
1 small onion, chopped

1 small bell pepper, chopped
Garlic powder to taste

Heat the black-eyed peas and add the rice. Add remaining ingredients and cook an additional 10 to 15 minutes. Do not overcook. This dish is best if the bell pepper and onion still have a crunch to them.

❧ ❧ ❧ **The Lady & Sons**

Mashed Potatoes with Sautéed Mushrooms

SERVES 6 TO 8

8 tablespoons (1 stick) butter
1 cup sliced fresh mushrooms
½ cup diced onion
2 tablespoons chopped fresh chives
1 clove garlic, chopped

1 cup white wine
6 cups (about 2 pounds) diced new
*   potatoes*
½ cup sour cream
Small amount whole milk

In a saucepan, melt butter and sauté mushrooms, onion, chives, and garlic. Add wine and simmer for about 15 minutes. In a pot, boil potatoes until done; drain. Combine all ingredients and mix. Whip until thick and creamy. Add milk for desired consistency.

Pineapple Casserole

SERVES 8

1 cup sugar
6 tablespoons all-purpose flour
2 cups grated sharp Cheddar cheese
Two 20-ounce cans pineapple
   chunks, drained (reserve
   6 tablespoons juice)

1 cup Ritz cracker crumbs
8 tablespoons (1 stick) butter,
   melted

Preheat oven to 350 degrees. In a mixing bowl, combine sugar and flour. Gradually stir in cheese. Add pineapple and stir well. Pour mixture into a greased casserole dish. Combine cracker crumbs, butter, and pineapple juice and spread on top of pineapple mixture. Bake for 25 to 30 minutes or until golden brown.   ❦ ❦ ❦ **The Lady & Sons**

Zucchini Custard Bake

SERVES 4 TO 6

4 tablespoons (½ stick) butter,
   melted
2 pounds zucchini, cut into small
   pieces
3 eggs
½ cup undiluted evaporated milk
   or light cream

2 tablespoons fine dry bread crumbs
1 teaspoon instant minced onion
1 teaspoon Worcestershire sauce
Dash of liquid hot pepper sauce
¾ teaspoon salt
⅛ teaspoon pepper
⅓ cup grated Parmesan cheese

Preheat oven to 350 degrees. In a large saucepan with a tight-fitting lid, combine melted butter and zucchini. Cover and cook over low heat, stirring occasionally, until tender (5 to 7 minutes). Remove from heat and set aside. Beat eggs with milk; add bread crumbs, onion, Worcestershire sauce, hot pepper sauce, salt, pepper, and 2 tablespoons of the Parmesan. Mix well. Combine mixture with zucchini, stirring until blended. Turn into a buttered 1½-quart casserole. Sprinkle top with remaining Parmesan cheese. Bake uncovered for 35 to 40 minutes. If the dish has been refrigerated, allow about 10 minutes longer baking time.

Rutabagas

SERVES 4 TO 6

Clint Eastwood was in for dinner one night while he was here in Savannah filming Midnight in the Garden of Good and Evil. *That particular night, we had rutabagas on the buffet. He made a point to tell me that he was a ten-year-old boy the last time he had tasted this wonderful vegetable. He said that he really enjoyed them again after all those years. Rutabagas are a winter vegetable, and not always available, so enjoy them while you can.*

1 chunk of streak-o'-lean
 (approximately ½ pound)
 (see Note)
Pinch of sugar

Salt and pepper to taste
1 rutabaga
2 tablespoons butter

Wash and cut streak-o'-lean to your liking. (You could use ham hock or smoked wings or even cut-up bacon, but I just prefer streak-o'-lean.) Place in a pot with enough water to cook meat. Add sugar, salt, and pepper. The water will cook out, so it might be necessary to add more during cooking. Cook meat while you prepare the rutabaga. Peel rutabaga and cut into cubes (as you would cut up potatoes for potato salad—about the same size). Add rutabaga to the meat; add more water if needed. Cover pot and cook until tender; this may take about 45 minutes. When done, remove from pot, add butter, and serve.

❧ ❧ ❧ *The Lady & Sons*

NOTE: Streak-o'-lean is very similar to bacon. You can get it from the butcher.

Breads

Zucchini Bread

The flavor improves with age and the bread keeps well frozen. You can also substitute pumpkin for zucchini.

3 ¼ cups all-purpose flour
1 ½ teaspoons salt
1 teaspoon ground nutmeg
2 teaspoons baking soda
1 teaspoon ground cinnamon
3 cups sugar

1 cup vegetable oil
4 eggs, beaten
⅔ cup water
2 cups grated zucchini
1 teaspoon lemon juice
1 cup chopped walnuts or pecans

Preheat oven to 350 degrees. Mix dry ingredients except for nuts in a large bowl. In a separate bowl, mix wet ingredients; fold into dry, and add nuts. Bake in two loaf pans for 1 hour, or until done.

Banana Nut Bread

YIELDS 1 LOAF

½ cup Crisco shortening
1 cup sugar
2 cups all-purpose flour
1 teaspoon salt
2 teaspoons baking powder

½ teaspoon baking soda
2 eggs, beaten
3 bananas, mashed
⅓ cup buttermilk
½ cup chopped walnuts or pecans

Preheat oven to 350 degrees. Cream shortening and sugar. Sift together flour, salt, baking powder, and baking soda and add to creamed mixture. Add remaining ingredients; mix well. Pour into a well-greased loaf pan. Bake for 40 to 45 minutes.

Easy Rolls

YIELDS 6 ROLLS

1 cup self-rising flour
½ cup milk

1 teaspoon sugar
2 tablespoons mayonnaise

Preheat oven to 350 degrees. Mix together flour and milk. Add sugar and mayonnaise. Pour into slightly greased muffin tins and bake for 12 to 15 minutes.

Pumpkin Bread

YIELDS 2 LOAVES

3 cups sugar
1 cup vegetable oil
4 eggs
2 cups canned pumpkin
⅔ cup water
3⅓ cups all-purpose flour

2 teaspoons baking soda
1½ teaspoons salt
1 teaspoon ground cinnamon
1 teaspoon ground nutmeg
½ to ¾ cup chopped pecans or
*   walnuts*

Preheat oven to 350 degrees. Grease and flour two loaf pans. Mix sugar and oil with mixer. Add eggs and blend. Add pumpkin and blend. Add water and blend. Combine remaining ingredients and add slowly. Fill pans equally and bake for 1 hour or until golden brown.

VARIATIONS: For the oil, substitute ½ cup oil and add ½ cup applesauce. For banana bread, substitute 2 cups mashed, ripe bananas for pumpkin and omit nutmeg.

Basic Biscuits

YIELDS APPROXIMATELY 3 DOZEN BISCUITS

1 package yeast	*1 tablespoon baking powder*
½ cup lukewarm water	*2 tablespoons sugar*
5 cups all-purpose flour	*¾ cup Crisco shortening*
1 teaspoon baking soda	*2 cups buttermilk*
1 teaspoon salt	

Preheat oven to 400 degrees. Dissolve yeast in warm water; set aside. Mix dry ingredients together. Cut in shortening. Add yeast and buttermilk and mix well. Turn dough onto lightly floured surface and roll out to desired thickness. Cut with small biscuit cutter and place on greased baking sheet. Bake for 12 minutes or until golden brown.

Hoecakes

YIELDS APPROXIMATELY 17 CAKES

These hoecakes have become a favorite with our guests. Use them to soak up that good pot liquor from turnip or collard greens. After the plate is completely sopped clean, save one to eat as a dessert along with maple syrup.

1 cup self-rising flour	*¾ cup buttermilk*
1 cup self-rising cornmeal	*⅓ cup plus 1 tablespoon water*
2 eggs	*¼ cup vegetable oil or bacon grease*
1 tablespoon sugar	*Oil or butter for frying*

Mix all ingredients well except for frying oil. Heat oil in a skillet over medium heat. Drop mixture by tablespoonfuls into hot skillet. Use approximately 2 tablespoons batter per hoecake. Brown until crisp; turn and brown on other side. Drain on paper towels. Leftover batter will keep in refrigerator for up to 2 days. ❦ ❦ ❦ **The Lady & Sons**

Corny Corn Bread

SERVES 8

1 cup self-rising cornmeal
¾ cup self-rising flour
½ cup vegetable oil plus ¼ cup for
  skillet
One 8-ounce can cream-style corn

2 eggs
1 cup sour cream
1 cup grated sharp Cheddar cheese
½ teaspoon cayenne pepper
  (optional)

Preheat oven to 375 degrees. Mix all ingredients together. Pour into a heated cast-iron skillet that has been well greased with oil. Bake until golden brown, approximately 30 minutes.

Pear Fritters

YIELDS APPROXIMATELY 21 PIECES

This fritter batter may be used for sliced fresh apples or bananas, or canned pineapple.

1 egg, beaten
½ cup milk
2 teaspoons sugar
1 teaspoon ground cinnamon
1 cup self-rising flour

1 cup sour cream
¼ cup vegetable oil
3 pears, peeled, cored, and sliced
  horizontally

Combine beaten egg, milk, sugar, cinnamon, and flour. Mix well and add sour cream. Heat 2 tablespoons oil to 375 degrees. Dip pears in batter, carefully place in oil, and cook 1 to 2 minutes. Turn and cook 1 to 2 minutes more. Add oil as needed. Remove fritters and drain. May be sprinkled with powdered sugar or cinnamon sugar. Serve warm.

Mother's Rolls

YIELDS APPROXIMATELY 2 DOZEN ROLLS

½ cup Crisco shortening
¼ cup sugar
1 heaping teaspoon salt
½ cup boiling water

1 package yeast
½ cup lukewarm water
1 egg
3 cups sifted all-purpose flour

Cream together shortening, sugar, and salt. Add boiling water. Dissolve yeast in ½ cup lukewarm water; beat egg and add. Combine with shortening and mix all together with flour. Beat well. Set aside at room temperature for 30 minutes, then refrigerate until needed. Preheat oven to 350 degrees. Roll out dough and cut into rolls. Place on greased cookie sheet. Bake for 15 minutes or until brown.

Sweet Blueberry Corn Bread

SERVES 8

1½ cups all-purpose flour
⅔ cup sugar
½ cup cornmeal
1 tablespoon baking powder
½ teaspoon salt
1¼ cups milk

2 large eggs, lightly beaten
⅓ cup canola oil
4 tablespoons butter, melted
1 cup blueberries, fresh or fresh
   frozen

Preheat oven to 350 degrees. Spray an 8-inch square baking pan with nonstick baking spray and set aside. In a medium mixing bowl, whisk together flour, sugar, cornmeal, baking powder, and salt. In a separate large mixing bowl, whisk together milk, eggs, oil, and butter. Add to flour mixture and stir just until blended. Gently fold in blueberries. Pour into prepared baking pan. Bake for 35 minutes, or until wooden pick comes out clean. Serve warm with butter.

Cheese Biscuits

YIELDS 8 LARGE BISCUITS

These biscuits have become one of our signature items at The Lady & Sons Restaurant. Everyone really looks forward to us bringing them out, whether it be after they are seated or while they are waiting in line.

2 cups self-rising flour
1 teaspoon baking powder
1 teaspoon sugar

⅓ cup Crisco shortening
¾ cup grated Cheddar cheese
1 cup buttermilk

Preheat oven to 350 degrees. Mix flour, baking powder, and sugar together using a fork; cut in shortening until it resembles cornmeal. Add cheese. Stir in buttermilk all at one time just until blended. Do not overstir. Drop by tablespoonfuls (I use an ice cream scoop to give biscuits a nicer shape) onto a well-greased baking sheet. Bake for 12 to 15 minutes.

GARLIC BUTTER

8 tablespoons (1 stick) butter,
    melted

2 cloves garlic, crushed

Combine butter and garlic over medium heat until butter absorbs garlic; brush over tops of warm biscuits. Store leftover butter for next baking.   🌿 🌿 🌿 *The Lady & Sons*

VARIATION: For breakfast, brush with plain butter or honey butter.

Cracklin' Corn Bread

YIELDS 4 PONES

1 cup cracklings
½ cup hot water
2 cups sifted yellow cornmeal

1 teaspoon salt
Small amount of cold water
Vegetable oil for skillet

Preheat oven to 425 degrees. Mash or break cracklings. Mix with hot water and pour into cornmeal; add salt. Use sufficient amount of cold water to make dough. Let stand 5 minutes. Shape into pones and place in a cast-iron skillet that has been heated with a few tablespoons of oil. Bake until brown, for about 15 minutes, then reduce heat to 350 degrees and bake for 30 to 45 minutes. The skillet should be placed near the top of the oven.

Dutch Bread

YIELDS 2 LOAVES

1 package yeast
½ cup warm water
2 tablespoons sugar
1½ teaspoons salt

6 cups all-purpose flour
2 cups scalded milk
2 tablespoons Crisco shortening

Preheat oven to 375 degrees. Mix yeast in water and set aside to dissolve. Combine dry ingredients. Add milk, shortening, and yeast. Pour into two greased 8 × 4 × 3-inch pans. Bake for approximately 45 to 50 minutes.

Bubba's Beer Biscuits

YIELDS 12 TO 16 BISCUITS

My brother Bubba confines most of his cooking to his charcoal grill, but he does come into the kitchen quite often to bake up these great biscuits.

4 cups Bisquick
¼ to ½ cup sugar

One 12-ounce can of beer
2 tablespoons butter, melted

Preheat oven to 400 degrees. Mix all ingredients well, adjusting the sugar according to how sweet a biscuit you prefer. Pour into well-greased muffin tins. Bake for 15 to 20 minutes. Serve with honey butter. 🌸 🌸 🌸 *The Lady & Sons*

Applesauce Bread

YIELDS 1 LOAF

2 cups all-purpose flour
¼ cup dark brown sugar
1 teaspoon baking powder
1 teaspoon baking soda
¾ teaspoon salt
1 teaspoon ground cinnamon
½ teaspoon ground nutmeg

1 teaspoon vanilla
8 tablespoons (1 stick) butter,
  softened
1 cup applesauce
2 eggs
1 cup raisins
½ cup chopped walnuts

Preheat oven to 350 degrees. Combine all ingredients except raisins and nuts. Mix well until blended. Stir in raisins and nuts. Pour into greased and floured 8 × 4 × 3-inch loaf pan. Bake for 60 to 65 minutes.

Homemade Yeast Donuts

YIELDS 1 DOZEN

¾ cup warm milk
¼ cup granulated sugar
1 packet active dry yeast
2½ cups all-purpose flour,
  plus extra for dusting dough
  and board
¼ teaspoon kosher salt
10 tablespoons butter,
  at room temperature

2 egg yolks
Peanut oil for frying
  (or vegetable oil)
2½ cups powdered sugar
2 teaspoons vanilla extract
4 tablespoons hot water
Sprinkles, for garnish

In the bowl of a standing mixer, add warm milk, sugar, and yeast. Let stand until yeast starts to foam, for about 10 minutes. Attach dough hook to mixer while yeast activates. In a medium mixing bowl, whisk together flour and salt. To the yeast mixture, add flour mixture, 2 tablespoons of the butter, and egg yolks and beat on medium speed for about 3 to 5 minutes, until dough comes together and forms a ball. Cover bowl and allow dough to rise in a warm place for 1 hour. Spray a sheet tray with nonstick cooking spray and set aside. Transfer dough to a lightly floured work surface and roll out to ½-inch thickness. Using a 2- to 3-inch donut cutter, cut out donuts and holes and transfer to the prepared sheet tray, spacing them 1 inch apart. Spray tops of donuts and holes with nonstick cooking spray and cover with plastic wrap. Let stand in a warm place until almost doubled in size, about 30 minutes. In a deep fryer or Dutch oven, heat oil to 350 degrees. Line a baking sheet with paper towels or brown paper and set aside. Working in batches, fry donuts and donut holes until light golden brown, about 1 minute per side. Transfer to the paper-lined baking sheet and let cool for 10 minutes before glazing. To make the glaze, in a large mixing bowl, using a hand mixer or whisk, combine remaining butter, powdered sugar, vanilla, and 4 tablespoons hot water. Mixture should be thin. Add more hot water if needed to thin glaze. Keep glaze warm until ready to use. Dip donuts, one at a time, into warm glaze, covering top half of each donut. Dip donuts, glazed side down, into a bowl of your favorite sprinkles and place donuts on a tray to rest for 10 minutes. Serve immediately.

NOTE: You can use a drinking glass or biscuit cutter to cut out donuts and a plastic bottle cap to cut out holes.

Herb Corn Bread

SERVES 9

1¼ cups self-rising cornmeal
¾ cup self-rising flour
1 teaspoon sugar
½ teaspoon dried marjoram
½ teaspoon dried thyme

¼ teaspoon celery seed
2 eggs, beaten
1¼ cups milk
6 tablespoons butter, melted

Preheat oven to 425 degrees. Combine dry ingredients in a large bowl. Combine eggs, milk, and butter. Add to dry ingredients, stirring until just moistened. Pour batter into a lightly greased 9-inch square pan. Bake for 25 minutes or until golden brown.

Peanut Butter Bread

YIELDS 1 LOAF

2 cups all-purpose flour
⅓ cup sugar
1 teaspoon salt

4 teaspoons baking powder
1½ cups milk
½ cup peanut butter

Preheat oven to 375 degrees. Combine dry ingredients. Add milk and peanut butter. Pour into a greased 8 × 4 × 3-inch loaf pan. Bake for approximately 50 minutes. Great with homemade jam.

Pineapple Cheese Bread

YIELDS 1 LOAF

2 cups self-rising flour
¾ cup sugar
1 cup canned crushed pineapple,
    with juice
2 eggs

2 tablespoons vegetable oil
¾ cup grated sharp Cheddar cheese
½ cup chopped walnuts
½ teaspoon pineapple extract

Preheat oven to 350 degrees. Sift flour into a large mixing bowl and add sugar. Mix together. In a separate bowl, mix pineapple, eggs, and oil and add to flour mixture, mixing well. Fold in cheese, nuts, and pineapple extract. Pour into a greased 9 × 3-inch loaf pan. Bake for 1 hour. Cool and turn out from pan, allowing to cool completely before slicing.

Sauces, Dressings, and Preserves

Daddy's Tangy Grilling Sauce

For good charcoal grilling, brush sauce over the meat during the last 10 or 15 minutes of grilling time. Turn often to prevent burning.

1 cup Worcestershire sauce
4 tablespoons (½ stick) butter

Juice of 2 lemons

Mix ingredients together and simmer for 10 minutes.

Chicken or Shrimp Marinade

YIELDS 1½ CUPS

3 cloves garlic, crushed
1½ teaspoons salt
½ cup packed brown sugar
3 tablespoons Dijon mustard
¼ cup apple cider vinegar

6 tablespoons olive oil
Juice of 1 lime
Juice of ½ lemon
Dash of cayenne or ground black
  pepper

Mix all ingredients with a whisk. Pour over chicken or shrimp. Refrigerate overnight. Grill over hot coals or broil in oven.

Spicy Barbecue Sauce

YIELDS 2 CUPS

1½ cups apple cider vinegar
1 to 2 tablespoons Worcestershire
   sauce
1 to 2 tablespoons peanut butter
1 teaspoon salt

Juice of 2 lemons
1 teaspoon pepper
2 tablespoons celery seed
2 tablespoons chili powder
4 tablespoons (½ stick) butter

Bring all ingredients to a boil until peanut butter dissolves. Stir to avoid sticking. Lower heat and simmer for 20 minutes.

The Lady's Barbecue Sauce

YIELDS 2 CUPS

½ cup oil
¼ cup lemon juice
1 teaspoon pepper
¾ cup ketchup
3 tablespoons brown sugar
Pinch of garlic salt or garlic
   powder

2 teaspoons salt
½ cup apple cider vinegar
3 tablespoons Worcestershire sauce
2 teaspoons paprika
¾ cup water
3 tablespoons prepared mustard
½ onion, finely chopped

Mix all ingredients together and simmer over medium heat for 15 minutes.　🍀 🍀 🍀 **The Lady & Sons**

Egg and Lemon Sauce

YIELDS 1 CUP

This is a tasty sauce that goes great with broccoli, cauliflower, asparagus, and fish.

3 eggs, separated
Juice of 2 lemons

1 tablespoon cornstarch
1 cup chicken stock

Beat egg whites until stiff; add egg yolks and continue beating. Add lemon juice slowly. Beat constantly to prevent curdling. Dissolve cornstarch in ¼ cup water; add to broth and cook over medium heat until it thickens. Slowly add hot stock to egg mixture, beating constantly. Sauce should be smooth and creamy.

Lemon Shrimp Cocktail Sauce

YIELDS ½ CUP

6 tablespoons mayonnaise
1 tablespoon horseradish
½ teaspoon grated onion

1 teaspoon prepared mustard
2 tablespoons lemon juice

Combine all ingredients and chill before serving. Serve with cold shrimp, crab claws, or raw oysters.

Savory Grilled Chicken Sauce

YIELDS 1½ CUPS

½ cup distilled vinegar
½ cup lemon juice
½ cup corn oil
1 tablespoon salt

¼ teaspoon ground black pepper
1½ tablespoons dry mustard
Sprinkle of cayenne pepper

Mix ingredients together. Bring to boil over medium heat. Stir frequently. Remove from heat; brush chicken with sauce while on the grill. Makes enough sauce for 2 chickens.

Lemon Butter for Fish

YIELDS ½ CUP

4 tablespoons (½ stick) butter
1 clove garlic, minced
2 tablespoons lemon juice

Dash of Worcestershire sauce
Salt and pepper to taste

Melt butter in a saucepan. Sauté garlic for 2 to 3 minutes. Add remaining ingredients and mix well. Serve warm over broiled fish.

Lemon Butter for Steak

YIELDS ½ CUP

2 tablespoons lemon juice
3 tablespoons butter
¼ teaspoon salt

¼ teaspoon paprika
1 tablespoon finely chopped fresh
    parsley

Combine all ingredients. Pour over cooked steaks and garnish with lemon wedges.

Sweet-and-Sour Dressing

YIELDS 3 CUPS

1½ cups vegetable oil
¾ cup vinegar
¾ cup sugar
1½ teaspoons salt

1½ teaspoons celery seed
1½ teaspoons dry mustard
1½ teaspoons paprika
1½ teaspoons grated onion

Combine all ingredients in a jar. Chill. Shake and serve over salad.

Poppy Seed Dressing

YIELDS 1¼ CUPS

⅓ cup honey
¼ cup red wine vinegar
1 tablespoon Dijon mustard
1 tablespoon minced onion

1 teaspoon House Seasoning
  (see page 180)
1 tablespoon poppy seeds
¾ cup olive oil

Combine ingredients except oil in a blender. Process on low, gradually adding oil. Chill; shake or stir before serving. ❦ ❦ ❦ *The Lady & Sons*

Aunt Peggy's Italian Dressing

YIELDS 2½ CUPS

4 cloves garlic, minced
½ teaspoon salt, or to taste
⅛ teaspoon pepper
¼ teaspoon dried basil
¼ teaspoon dried oregano
½ teaspoon paprika
⅛ teaspoon dried dill

Pinch of dill seed
½ teaspoon sugar
½ teaspoon grated Parmesan cheese
1 teaspoon lemon juice
1¾ cups vinegar
¾ cup olive oil

Combine all ingredients and mix well.

Honey Mustard Dressing

YIELDS 1¼ CUPS

¾ cup mayonnaise
3 tablespoons honey
2 tablespoons yellow mustard
1 tablespoon lemon juice or juice
   from ½ lemon

Horseradish to taste
2 tablespoons orange juice (more
   or less as needed)

Combine all ingredients except orange juice; stir well. Thin to pouring consistency with orange juice. Cover and chill for 2 to 3 hours.

🍀 🍀 🍀 *The Lady & Sons*

Buttermilk Dressing

YIELDS 2 CUPS

½ cup sour cream
1 cup mayonnaise
½ cup buttermilk
1 teaspoon House Seasoning
   (see page 180)

2 tablespoons minced fresh parsley
1 tablespoon minced onion

Mix ingredients together and chill overnight.

🍀 🍀 🍀 *The Lady & Sons*

Pear Honey

YIELDS 12 TO 16 HALF-PINT JARS

One 20-ounce can crushed
   pineapple with syrup
8 cups (about 3 pounds) peeled,
   cored, and chopped pears

10 cups sugar
1 tablespoon lemon juice

Mix all ingredients and cook until pears are tender and mixture thickens, approximately 30 minutes. Place in sterilized jars and seal while still hot.

Mint Julep Jelly

YIELDS 4 TO 5 HALF-PINT JARS

1½ cups bourbon
½ cup water
3 cups sugar

6 tablespoons Certo
4 to 5 fresh mint sprigs

Combine bourbon, water, and sugar in double boiler over medium heat. Stir until sugar is dissolved. Remove from heat; add Certo. Pour into sterilized jars. Add mint sprig to each jar and seal.

Port Wine Jelly

YIELDS 5 HALF-PINT JARS

1 cup port wine
1 cup cranberry juice

3½ cups sugar
½ bottle Certo

Stir wine, juice, and sugar together in double boiler over medium heat until sugar is dissolved. Remove from heat and add Certo. Pour into sterilized jars and seal immediately.

Strawberry Fig Preserves

YIELDS 8 HALF-PINT JARS

3 cups mashed ripe figs
3 cups sugar

Two 3-ounce packages strawberry
Jell-O

Mix all ingredients together in saucepan and cook 4 minutes at rolling boil. Stir frequently. Skim. Pour into sterilized jars; seal.

Pepper Jelly

YIELDS 6 HALF-PINT JARS

¾ cup chopped green bell pepper
¼ cup chopped fresh hot green
   pepper
1½ cups apple vinegar

6 cups sugar
4 ounces Certo
4 drops green food coloring

Process bell and hot pepper in food processor, then mix all ingredients except Certo and food coloring. Bring to rolling boil. Remove from heat and add Certo and coloring. Pour into sterilized jars and seal.

Honey Butter

YIELDS 1 CUP

½ pound (2 sticks) butter

2 tablespoons honey

Allow butter to soften slightly at room temperature. Using an electric mixer, whip butter and honey together in a bowl until well mixed.
   To give the butter an extra flair, you can:

- put the mixture in a butter mold and allow to chill;
- roll butter up in wax paper, allow it to chill, and slice when ready to use;
- spread softened butter in a shallow pan, chill, and, when it is firm, use a miniature cookie cutter to make different shapes;
- run semichilled butter through a pastry bag, using a star tip.

You can also adapt the above to suit your needs. For example, you could add fresh strawberries, blueberries, peaches, or other fruit. Fresh herbs like basil, thyme, and oregano—as well as fresh garlic—help make wonderful herbed butter (for this you should omit the honey).

❧ ❧ ❧ *The Lady & Sons*

Desserts

COOKIES AND BROWNIES

OTHER CONFECTIONS

Caramel Apple Cake with Caramel Topping

SERVES 15 TO 20

2 ½ cups sugar
3 eggs
1 ½ cups vegetable oil
3 cups all-purpose flour

2 teaspoons vanilla
1 cup chopped walnuts
2 ½ cups diced apples, canned or
    fresh

Preheat oven to 350 degrees. Cream together sugar, eggs, and oil. Add flour; mix together until well blended. Add vanilla, nuts, and diced apples. Spread into a lightly greased and floured 13 × 9-inch baking dish; bake for 45 to 60 minutes. Cake is done when toothpick inserted in center comes out clean. When cake is done, punch holes in it with a knife and pour topping over.

CARAMEL TOPPING

¾ pound (3 sticks) butter
2 cups brown sugar

¼ cup milk

Heat all ingredients together over medium heat. Bring to boil, stirring constantly. Let boil for about 2 minutes. Pour over warm cake.

❦ ❦ ❦ *The Lady & Sons*

Rum Cake

SERVES 12 TO 16

1 cup chopped walnuts
One 18 ¼-ounce package yellow
  cake mix
One 3 ½-ounce package instant
  vanilla pudding mix

4 eggs
½ cup buttermilk
½ cup vegetable oil
½ cup dark rum

Preheat oven to 325 degrees. Grease and flour a 10-inch tube pan. Sprinkle nuts over bottom of pan. Mix remaining ingredients together. Pour batter over nuts. Bake for 1 hour. Cool. Invert on service plate. Prick top with fork or toothpick. Drizzle and smooth glaze evenly over top and sides. Allow cake to absorb glaze. Use all the glaze.

GLAZE

4 tablespoons (½ stick) butter
¼ cup water

1 cup sugar
½ cup dark rum

Melt butter in saucepan. Stir in water and sugar. Boil 5 minutes, stirring constantly. Remove from heat; stir in rum.

Coconut Cake

SERVES 12 TO 16

*One 18¼-ounce package yellow
pudding cake mix*
1 cup sour cream

1½ cups sugar
*12 ounces canned or frozen
shredded coconut*

Preheat oven to 350 degrees. Make cake by following directions on package, substituting milk for water. Divide and bake in three 9-inch round cake pans for 20 minutes. Remove from oven and allow to cool for 5 minutes. Remove from pans. Stir together sour cream, sugar, and coconut. Spread between slightly warm cake layers, piercing each layer as you stack them. Store cake in container in refrigerator for 2 to 3 days. This allows cake to soak up moisture from the coconut. On the third day, prepare icing for cake.

ICING

2 unbeaten egg whites
1½ cups sugar
*2 teaspoons light corn syrup, or ¼
teaspoon cream of tartar*
⅓ cup cold water

Dash of salt
1 teaspoon vanilla
*Additional coconut to top icing
(about ½ cup)*

Place all ingredients except vanilla and additional coconut in top of double boiler, but do not place over heat; beat 1 minute with electric hand mixer. Place over boiling water and cook, beating constantly, until frosting forms stiff peaks (about 7 minutes). Remove from boiling water; add vanilla and beat until it reaches spreading consistency (about 2 minutes). Frost top and sides of cake; sprinkle with additional coconut. Cover and store at room temperature.

Chocolate Strawberry Shortcake

SERVES 15 TO 20

2 cups cake flour
1½ cups sugar
⅔ cup cocoa
½ cup Crisco shortening
1½ cups buttermilk
1½ teaspoons baking soda
1 teaspoon salt

1 teaspoon vanilla
2 whole eggs or 3 egg whites
1 quart fresh strawberries, rinsed
   and sliced
1 cup whipped cream or
   Cool Whip

Preheat oven to 350 degrees. In a mixing bowl, combine all ingredients in order listed, except strawberries and whipping cream. Beat with mixer on low speed, scraping bowl constantly, for 30 seconds. Beat on high speed, scraping bowl occasionally, for 3 minutes. Pour into greased and floured 13 × 9-inch pan. Bake for 30 to 35 minutes. Cool cake completely. Cut into squares. Place 2 or 3 squares in dessert cups and layer with small amount of strawberries and whipped cream. Garnish with strawberries. *A heavenly treat!*

Chocolate Chip Nut Cake

SERVES 16 TO 20

½ cup Crisco shortening
½ pound (2 sticks) butter
2¾ cups sugar
6 large eggs
3 cups all-purpose flour
1 teaspoon baking powder

1 cup milk
1 teaspoon vanilla
One 12-ounce package semisweet
   chocolate chips
1½ cups chopped pecans or walnuts

Cream shortening, butter, and sugar. Add eggs, one at a time, beating thoroughly after each. Sift flour with baking powder. Add to creamed mixture, alternating with milk. Roll nuts and chocolate chips in a little flour and add to mixture, then add vanilla. Pour into a greased and floured tube pan. Place in cold oven and bake at 325 degrees for about 1½ hours, or until done.

Low-Fat Peach Cake

SERVES 12 TO 16

¼ teaspoon sugar

1 teaspoon ground cinnamon

CAKE

2 cups all-purpose flour
1½ cups sugar
½ cup Crisco shortening
½ cup milk
One 15-ounce can cling peaches,
drained (reserve ½ cup juice)

3 egg whites
3½ teaspoons baking powder
½ teaspoon ground cinnamon
1 teaspoon vanilla
1 teaspoon salt

Preheat oven to 350 degrees. Use no-stick cooking spray in Bundt pan. Mix together sugar and cinnamon. Sprinkle mixture over bottom and sides of pan. Combine all cake ingredients together, including reserved juice. Beat with mixer on low speed for 30 seconds, scraping bowl constantly. Beat on high speed for 2 minutes. Pour into Bundt pan. Bake for 40 to 45 minutes. Remove from oven; cool completely. Frost with icing immediately before serving.

ICING

One 6-ounce container nonfat
peach yogurt

One 8-ounce container Lite
Cool Whip

Mix together. Frost cake.

Savannah Chocolate Cake
with Hot Fudge Sauce

SERVES APPROXIMATELY 20

2 cups brown sugar
½ cup Crisco shortening
1 cup buttermilk
1 teaspoon vanilla
2 ounces unsweetened chocolate,
  melted

3 eggs
2 cups sifted all-purpose flour
1 teaspoon baking soda
½ teaspoon salt

Preheat oven to 350 degrees. Cream together brown sugar and shortening; add buttermilk and vanilla. Add melted chocolate, then add eggs one at a time; beat for 2 minutes. Sift together flour, baking soda, and salt and add to creamed mixture. Beat an additional 2 minutes. Pour into a 13 × 9 × 2-inch greased, floured pan. Bake for 40 to 45 minutes.

HOT FUDGE SAUCE

One 4-ounce bar German
  chocolate
½ ounce unsweetened chocolate
8 tablespoons (1 stick) butter

3 cups powdered sugar
1⅔ cups evaporated milk
1¼ teaspoons vanilla

Melt chocolate and butter in saucepan over very low heat. Stir in powdered sugar, alternating with evaporated milk, blending well. Bring to a boil over medium heat, stirring constantly. Cook and stir until mixture becomes thick and creamy, about 8 minutes. Stir in vanilla; serve warm over Savannah Chocolate Cake (or your favorite sheet cake).

Mama's Pound Cake

SERVES 16 TO 20

½ pound (2 sticks) butter
½ cup Crisco shortening
3 cups sugar
5 eggs
3 cups all-purpose flour

½ teaspoon salt
½ teaspoon baking powder
1 cup milk
1 teaspoon vanilla

Preheat oven to 325 degrees. Cream butter and shortening together. Add sugar, a little at a time. Add eggs, one at a time, beating after each. Sift together dry ingredients and add to mixture alternately with milk, starting with flour and ending with flour. Add vanilla. Pour into greased and floured tube pan and bake for 1½ hours.

Grandmother Paul's Sour Cream Pound Cake

SERVES 16 TO 20

½ pound (2 sticks) butter
3 cups sugar
1 cup sour cream
3 cups all-purpose flour

½ teaspoon baking soda
6 eggs
1 teaspoon vanilla

Preheat oven to 325 degrees. Cream butter and sugar together; add sour cream. Sift flour and baking soda together. Add to creamed mixture, alternately with eggs, one at a time, beating after each. Add vanilla. Pour into a greased and floured tube pan and bake for 1 hour 20 minutes.   ❦ ❦ ❦ **The Lady & Sons**

Luscious Lime Cheesecake

SERVES 15 TO 20

One 18¼-ounce package yellow
  cake mix
4 eggs
¼ cup vegetable oil
Two 8-ounce packages cream cheese,
  at room temperature
One 14-ounce can sweetened
  condensed milk

2 teaspoons grated lime zest
⅓ cup fresh lime juice
1 teaspoon vanilla
One 8-ounce container Cool Whip,
  or 2 cups heavy cream, whipped
  with ½ cup sugar until stiff
Lime slices, for garnish

Preheat oven to 300 degrees. Reserve ½ cup dry cake mix. In large bowl, combine remaining cake mix, 1 egg, and oil. Mix well (mixture will be crumbly). Press evenly in bottom and 1½ inches up sides of greased 13 × 9-inch pan. In same bowl, beat cheese until fluffy. Beat in condensed milk until smooth. Add remaining eggs and reserved cake mix and beat 1 minute at medium speed. Stir in lime zest, lime juice, and vanilla. Pour into prepared crust. Bake for 50 to 55 minutes or until center is firm. Cool to room temperature. Chill thoroughly. Spread Cool Whip over top. Cut into squares to serve. Garnish with lime slices.

Gooey Butter Cakes

SERVES 15 TO 20

I could write a full chapter on this dessert. It is the number-one choice in our restaurant.

One 18¼-ounce package yellow
   cake mix
1 egg

8 tablespoons (1 stick) butter,
   melted

Preheat oven to 350 degrees. Combine ingredients and mix well. Pat into a lightly greased 13 × 9-inch baking pan. Prepare filling.

FILLING

One 8-ounce package cream
   cheese, softened
2 eggs
1 teaspoon vanilla

8 tablespoons (1 stick) butter,
   melted
One 16-ounce box powdered sugar

Beat cream cheese until smooth. Add eggs and vanilla. Add butter; beat. Add powdered sugar and mix well. Spread over cake mixture. Bake for 40 to 50 minutes. You want the center to be a little gooey, so do not overbake.

VARIATIONS:

1. For the holidays, add a 15-ounce can of pumpkin to the filling; add cinnamon and nutmeg.
2. Add a 20-ounce can of drained crushed pineapple to the filling.
3. Use a lemon cake mix. Add lemon juice and zest to the filling.
4. Use a chocolate cake mix with cream cheese filling. Add chocolate chips and nuts on top.
5. Use a spiced carrot cake mix. Add chopped nuts and shredded carrots to the filling.
6. Use mandarin oranges, bananas, blueberries, or strawberries—just coordinate your extract flavorings.
7. Use a chocolate cake mix. Add ¾ to 1 cup peanut butter and nuts to the filling.

❧ ❧ ❧ *The Lady & Sons*

Grandmother Paul's Red Velvet Cake

SERVES 16 TO 20

2 eggs
2 cups sugar
1 teaspoon cocoa
2 ounces red food coloring
½ pound (2 sticks) butter
2½ cups cake flour

1 teaspoon salt
1 cup buttermilk
1 teaspoon vanilla
½ teaspoon baking soda
1 tablespoon vinegar

Preheat oven to 350 degrees. Beat eggs; add sugar. Mix cocoa and food coloring. Add butter and egg mixture; mix well. Sift together flour and salt. Add to creamed mixture alternately with buttermilk. Blend in vanilla. In a small bowl, combine soda and vinegar and add to mixture. Pour into three 9-inch round greased and floured pans. Bake for 20 to 25 minutes, or until tests done.

ICING

2 egg whites
1½ cups sugar
5 tablespoons cold water
2 tablespoons light corn syrup

1 cup miniature marshmallows
1 cup or 3½-ounce can shredded
coconut
1 cup chopped pecans

Cook egg whites, sugar, water, and corn syrup in double boiler for 5 minutes and beat. Add marshmallows; stir until melted. Fold in coconut and nuts. Spread between layers and on top and sides of cooled cake.   ❧ ❧ ❧ *The Lady & Sons*

Cheesecake

SERVES 10 TO 12

1 cup graham cracker crumbs	*4 tablespoons (½ stick) butter,*
¼ cup sugar	*melted*

Preheat oven to 350 degrees. Mix ingredients together and pat onto bottom and sides of an 8-inch springform cake pan. Prepare filling.

FILLING

2 eggs	*1 cup sugar*
12 ounces cream cheese, softened	*½ teaspoon vanilla*

Beat eggs and softened cream cheese together. Add sugar and vanilla. Beat until well blended. Pour into prepared crust. Bake for 25 to 30 minutes. Let cool for 10 minutes. Add topping.

TOPPING

½ cup sugar	*½ teaspoon vanilla*
1 cup sour cream	

Combine ingredients and put on top of cake; return to oven for 10 minutes.

OPTIONAL FRESH FRUIT TOPPING

2 cups fresh raspberries, blueberries,	*¾ cup water*
strawberries, cherries, etc.	*1 tablespoon butter*
½ cup sugar	*2 tablespoons cornstarch*

In small saucepan, bring fruit, sugar, ½ cup water, and butter to a boil. Mix cornstarch and ¼ cup water together. Add to boiling pot, cooking and stirring constantly for 1 minute or until thick. Cool to room temperature. Serve dollop on each slice of cheesecake, with a sprig of fresh mint for garnish. ❦ ❦ ❦ *The Lady & Sons*

NOTE: You can use a canned pie filling (blueberry, strawberry, or cherry) instead of fresh fruit.

Pineapple Cake

SERVES 16 TO 20

One 16-ounce can crushed
    pineapple in heavy syrup
2 cups Bisquick
1 cup sifted all-purpose flour
1 teaspoon baking soda
1 cup sugar

¾ cup sour cream
8 tablespoons (1 stick) butter
2 teaspoons vanilla
2 large eggs
2 tablespoons rum

Preheat oven to 350 degrees. Drain pineapple well, reserving syrup for glaze. Stir Bisquick, flour, and baking soda together and set aside. Beat sugar, sour cream, butter, and vanilla together for 2 minutes. Add eggs and beat 1 additional minute. Add flour mixture and beat 1 minute longer. Mix in drained pineapple and rum. Pour into well-greased 9-inch Bundt pan. Bake for about 45 minutes or until cake tests done. Remove from oven and spoon about half the glaze over cake. Let stand 10 minutes and then turn onto serving plate. Spoon on remaining glaze. Cool before cutting.

GLAZE

¾ cup sugar
4 tablespoons butter

¼ cup reserved pineapple syrup
2 tablespoons rum (optional)

Combine sugar, butter, and syrup. Stir over low heat until sugar is dissolved and butter is melted. Remove from heat and add rum, if desired. 🍀 🍀 🍀 *The Lady & Sons*

Chocolate Sheet Cake

SERVES 15 TO 20

2 cups sugar
½ teaspoon salt
2 cups all-purpose flour
8 tablespoons (1 stick) butter
½ cup vegetable oil
1 cup water

¼ cup cocoa
2 eggs
1 teaspoon baking soda
½ cup buttermilk
1 teaspoon vanilla

Preheat oven to 350 degrees. Combine sugar, salt, and flour in a large mixing bowl. In a saucepan, bring to a boil butter, oil, water, and cocoa. Add to flour mixture. Beat eggs, baking soda, buttermilk, and vanilla. Add to dry ingredients. Pour into greased and floured 13 × 9 × 2-inch pan. Bake for 25 minutes.

ICING

8 tablespoons (1 stick) butter
3 tablespoons cocoa
6 tablespoons milk

1 teaspoon vanilla
One 16-ounce box powdered sugar
1 cup chopped pecans or walnuts

Melt together butter and cocoa. Add milk and vanilla. Stir in powdered sugar and nuts. Spread on warm cake. 🌿 🌿 🌿 *The Lady & Sons*

Banana Split Cake

SERVES 15 TO 20

2 cups crushed graham crackers
¾ pound (3 sticks) butter
2 eggs, or 2 pasteurized eggs
One 16-ounce box powdered sugar

One 20-ounce can crushed
   pineapple, drained
2 to 3 bananas, sliced
One 12-ounce container Cool Whip

For crust, mix crushed graham crackers and 1 stick of butter. Line bottom and sides of a 13 × 9-inch pan with mixture. Beat until fluffy eggs, 2 sticks butter, and the powdered sugar. Spread mixture on crust. Add layer of crushed pineapple (drained) and layer of sliced bananas. Cover with Cool Whip. Sprinkle with nuts or graham crackers. Refrigerate for 1 hour.   🍀 🍀 🍀 **The Lady & Sons**

Grandmama Hiers's Carrot Cake

SERVES 16 TO 20

2 cups all-purpose flour
2 cups sugar
2 teaspoons baking soda
2 teaspoons cinnamon
1 teaspoon salt

4 eggs
1½ cups vegetable oil
3 cups grated carrots
1½ cups chopped pecans (optional)

Preheat oven to 350 degrees. In a large bowl, combine flour, sugar, baking soda, cinnamon, and salt. Add eggs and vegetable oil and mix well; add carrots and pecans. Pour into three 9-inch round greased, floured pans. Bake for approximately 40 minutes. Remove from oven and cool for 5 minutes. Remove from pans, place on waxpaper, and allow to cool completely before frosting.

FROSTING

One 8-ounce package cream cheese
8 tablespoons (1 stick) butter
One 16-ounce box powdered sugar

1 teaspoon vanilla
½ cup chopped pecans

Combine all ingredients except for nuts and beat until fluffy. Stir in nuts. Frost cake.   🍀 🍀 🍀 **The Lady & Sons**

Tunnel of Fudge Cake

SERVES 16 TO 20

¾ pound (3 sticks) butter
6 eggs
1½ cups sugar
One 12-ounce can creamy
   chocolate frosting

2 cups all-purpose flour
2 cups chopped walnuts or pecans

Preheat oven to 350 degrees. Cream butter in large bowl on high speed. Add eggs one at a time, beating well. Add sugar gradually, creaming at high speed, until light and fluffy. Gradually add flour. By hand, stir in frosting mix and nuts until well blended. Pour batter in well-greased and floured Bundt pan. Bake for 60 to 65 minutes. Cool 2 hours before removing from pan. Cake will have a dry, brownie-type crust and a moist center with a tunnel of fudge running through it.

Better Than Sex? Yes!

SERVES 15 TO 20

One 18½-ounce package chocolate
   cake mix
One 14-ounce can sweetened
   condensed milk

One 6-ounce jar caramel or hot
   fudge topping
8 ounces Cool Whip
4 Skor candy bars, crushed

Prepare cake according to directions and bake in 9 × 13-inch pan. Pierce warm cake all over with toothpick. Pour milk over cake. Pour caramel over cake. Chill. Before serving, top with whipped topping and sprinkle with crushed candy.   ❧ ❧ ❧ **The Lady & Sons**

Old-Time Lemon "Cheesecake"

SERVES 16 TO 20

While the recipe contains no actual cheese, Southerners have referred to this dessert as lemon cheesecake for generations. Go figure!

1½ sticks butter
2 cups sugar
3½ cups all-purpose flour
3½ teaspoons baking powder

1 cup milk
1 teaspoon vanilla
6 egg whites, beaten to stiff peaks

Preheat oven to 375 degrees. Cream butter; add sugar. Sift flour and baking powder together three times and add to butter alternately with milk and vanilla. Fold in egg whites. Bake in three greased 8-inch round pans for 35 minutes.

ICING

9 egg yolks
1½ cups sugar

¾ pound (3 sticks) butter
Juice and zest of 4 lemons

Mix all ingredients together and cook in double boiler until thick, approximately 20 minutes. Allow cake to cool. Spread icing in between layers and on entire outside of cake.

Punch Bowl Cake

SERVES 16 TO 20

One 18¼-ounce package yellow
   cake mix
Two 3½-ounce packages instant
   vanilla pudding mix
   (prepared according to
   instructions on box)
One 20-ounce can crushed
   pineapple, drained
6 medium bananas, sliced

2 pints strawberries (crush one
   pint, slice one pint, and mix
   both together)
One 24-ounce container Cool
   Whip (thawed), or fresh
   whipped cream (1 quart heavy
   cream whipped with 1 cup
   sugar till stiff)

Prepare cake in two 9-inch round pans according to directions. Put one layer of cake in the bottom of a punch bowl. Add half of the pudding, half of the pineapple, 3 sliced bananas, half of the strawberries, and half of the Cool Whip. Put another layer of cake in punch bowl along with remaining pudding, pineapple, bananas, and strawberries. Top off with Cool Whip and sprinkle strawberry juice on top.

Chocolate Pound Cake

SERVES 16 TO 20

3 cups sugar
½ pound (2 sticks) butter
½ cup vegetable shortening
5 eggs
3 cups all-purpose flour
4 tablespoons cocoa

½ teaspoon salt
½ teaspoon baking powder
½ teaspoon baking soda
1 cup buttermilk
1 tablespoon vanilla

Preheat oven to 350 degrees. Mix sugar with butter and vegetable shortening; add eggs one at a time, beating after each. Mix together dry ingredients. Add dry ingredients alternately with milk to butter mixture, beginning with flour and ending with flour. Add vanilla. Bake in a greased and floured tube pan for about 1 hour.

Easy Coffee Cake

SERVES 12 TO 15

Two 8-ounce cans refrigerated
    crescent rolls
1 cup sugar
Two 8-ounce packages cream
    cheese, softened

1 teaspoon vanilla
1 egg, separated
½ cup chopped pecans

Preheat oven to 350 degrees. Spread one can of crescent rolls in bottom of 13 × 9-inch pan. Cream together ¾ cup sugar, cream cheese, vanilla, and egg yolk. Spread mixture over rolls. Top with second package of crescent roll dough. Beat egg white until frothy and spread on top. Sprinkle top with remaining sugar and nuts. Bake for 30 to 35 minutes.

Applesauce Cupcakes

YIELDS APPROXIMATELY 2 DOZEN

1 egg
2 cups all-purpose flour
½ teaspoon ground cloves
¼ teaspoon salt
1½ teaspoons ground nutmeg
1 teaspoon ground cinnamon
1½ sticks butter, melted

1 teaspoon vanilla
1 cup chopped pecans
1½ cups sugar
1 cup raisins
1½ cups hot applesauce with
    2 teaspoons baking soda added

Preheat oven to 350 degrees. Mix above ingredients in bowl by hand except for applesauce. Last, add hot applesauce and baking soda. Pour batter into paper-lined cupcake pans. Bake for 25 minutes or until done.

Chocolate Damnation

SERVES 15 TO 20

One 19.8-ounce package brownie
   mix
12 ounces semisweet chocolate
¼ cup strong black brewed coffee

2 eggs, separated
¼ cup coffee liqueur
3 tablespoons sugar
¼ cup heavy cream

Prepare brownie batter according to directions on box. Pour into a greased 13 × 9 × 2-inch pan. Bake according to instructions on box. When cool, cut into squares and remove from pan. Clean pan thoroughly and grease once more. Place brownies back in greased pan. Combine chocolate and coffee in top of double boiler, and melt over boiling water. Remove from heat. Beat egg yolks and stir in small amount of chocolate mixture; pour mixture into balance of chocolate mixture; stir until smooth. Stir in liqueur and set aside to cool. Beat egg whites until foamy; gradually add sugar and beat until stiff. Whip cream until stiff. Fold cream into chocolate mixture; fold in egg whites. Pour filling over brownies. Cover with plastic wrap and chill 3 to 4 hours, until firm. Invert onto serving platter and drizzle on glaze. Let set and decorate with chocolate curls, if desired.

CHOCOLATE GLAZE

4 ounces semisweet chocolate

3 tablespoons strong black brewed
   coffee

Combine chocolate and coffee in double boiler. Heat until melted. Stir well.

Peanut Butter Cake

SERVES 12 TO 16

1 cup all-purpose flour
1 cup plus 2 tablespoons sugar
3½ teaspoons baking powder
¾ teaspoon salt
2 cups graham cracker crumbs
Peanut butter to taste (at least
    ½ cup; if using more, decrease
    shortening by an equal amount)

¾ cup Crisco shortening
1 cup plus 2 tablespoons milk
1½ teaspoons vanilla
3 eggs

Preheat oven to 375 degrees. Sift flour, sugar, baking powder, and salt together. Add graham cracker crumbs, peanut butter, shortening, milk, and vanilla. Beat mixture with electric mixer on low until moistened, then beat on medium for 2 minutes. Add eggs and beat for 1 minute. Bake in a greased 9 × 13-inch pan for 30 to 35 minutes. Do not remove from pan.

FROSTING

2 cups sugar
½ cup cocoa

8 tablespoons (1 stick) butter
½ cup milk

Mix all ingredients together. Heat in a saucepan and bring to a boil. Boil for 1 minute. Cool slightly. With a wooden spoon handle, poke a few holes in the cake, then pour warm frosting over it.

❦ ❦ ❦ **The Lady & Sons**

French Coconut Pie

SERVES 6 TO 8

4 tablespoons (½ stick) butter
2 eggs, beaten
1 tablespoon all-purpose flour
¾ cup sugar

1 cup or 3½-ounce can shredded
  coconut
1 cup milk
One 9-inch unbaked pie shell

Preheat oven to 400 degrees. Melt butter; add remaining ingredients. Pour into pie shell. Bake until firm, about 45 to 60 minutes.

Butterscotch Pie

SERVES 6 TO 8

¾ cup brown sugar
5 tablespoons all-purpose flour
½ teaspoon salt
2 cups milk

2 egg yolks, lightly beaten
2 tablespoons butter
1 teaspoon vanilla
One 9-inch prebaked pie shell

Combine sugar, flour, and salt and stir in milk slowly. Cook in double boiler over boiling water until thickened, stirring constantly. Cover and cook 10 minutes longer, stirring occasionally. Add small amount of hot mixture to egg yolks, stirring rigorously. Add back to pot and cook 1 minute longer. Add butter and vanilla and cool. Place filling in pastry shell and cover with whipped cream or meringue.

Corrie's Kentucky Pie

SERVES 16 TO 22

4 eggs, lightly beaten
2 cups sugar
One 12-ounce package semisweet
    chocolate chips, melted
1 cup sifted self-rising flour
½ pound (2 sticks) butter, melted

2 teaspoons vanilla
2 cups chopped pecans
Two 9-inch unbaked deep-dish
    pie shells or 3 regular 9-inch
    unbaked pie shells

Preheat oven to 350 degrees. Combine eggs, sugar, and melted chocolate in large bowl. Add flour and mix well; stir in remaining ingredients except for pie shells. Spread mixture into pie shells. Bake for 30 minutes. Serve warm with ice cream. Freezes well!

Mini Pecan Pies

YIELDS 24

8 tablespoons (1 stick) butter
1 cup all-purpose flour

One 3-ounce package cream cheese

Preheat oven to 325 degrees. Soften cheese and butter and blend well. Stir in flour. Chill 1 hour. Shape into twenty-four 1-inch balls. Place in ungreased small muffin tins. Press down to form crust.

FILLING

1 egg
¾ cup brown sugar
1 tablespoon butter

1 teaspoon vanilla
Dash of salt
⅔ cup chopped pecans

Beat egg, sugar, butter, vanilla, and salt until smooth. Divide half the nuts among pastry cups. Add egg mixture. Top with remaining nuts. Bake for 25 minutes or until filling hardens.

Praline Pumpkin Pie

SERVES 6 TO 8

⅓ cup finely chopped pecans
⅓ cup plus ½ cup brown sugar
2 tablespoons butter, softened
One 9-inch unbaked pie shell
3 whole eggs
2 eggs, separated
1 cup canned pumpkin
1½ cups heavy cream

¼ cup dark rum
½ teaspoon salt
1 teaspoon ground cinnamon
¼ teaspoon ground cloves
¼ teaspoon ground ginger
¼ teaspoon ground mace
   (optional)
2 tablespoons granulated sugar

Preheat oven to 400 degrees. Blend pecans with ⅓ cup brown sugar and softened butter. Press gently with the back of a spoon into bottom of pie shell. Blend all remaining ingredients except egg whites and granulated sugar. Pour into pie shell. Bake for about 50 minutes. Make a meringue by beating egg whites until stiff, adding the granulated sugar while beating. After pie has baked, remove from oven and cover with meringue. Return to 425-degree oven just to brown meringue.

Chocolate Chip Pie

SERVES 6 TO 8

2 eggs
½ cup all-purpose flour
½ cup packed brown sugar
½ cup granulated sugar
8 tablespoons (1 stick) butter,
   melted

One 6-ounce package semisweet
   chocolate chips
1 cup chopped pecans or walnuts
One 9-inch unbaked pie shell
Whipped topping (optional)

Preheat oven to 325 degrees. In large bowl, beat eggs until foamy. Add flour and brown sugar; beat until well blended. Blend in granulated sugar and butter. Stir in chocolate chips and nuts. Pour into pie shell. Bake for 1 hour. Cover with whipped topping, if desired.

Nita's Secret Peach Pie

SERVES 6

Savannah native Nita McDougald was always a lady. Like all ladies of her time, she knew how to keep a secret, especially about her pies. Luckily for us, her daughter Brenda—also a lady—can't keep a secret.

1 prepared pastry for 9-inch
   two-crust pie
7 cups peaches, fresh, peeled and
   thickly sliced (or frozen slices)
Juice of ½ lemon
1½ cups sugar

¼ cup flour
½ teaspoon almond extract
¼ teaspoon nutmeg
5 tablespoons butter, divided
1 egg
1 tablespoon water

Preheat oven to 425 degrees. Roll out one-half of pie dough to fit bottom of 9-inch pie pan, allowing a 1-inch overhang, and place in refrigerator until ready to use. In a large sauce pan, place peaches, lemon juice, sugar, and flour and stir until coated. Bring fruit mixture to a low boil. Reduce heat to low and cook until fruit is just slightly tender. Remove pan from heat. Stir in almond extract, nutmeg, and three tablespoons of the butter. Allow to cool slightly. Remove pie pan from refrigerator and fill with cooled mixture. Dot top of fruit with remaining two tablespoons of the butter. Roll out the second crust and cover top of pie with lattice top or any style of crust you like. (If covering completely, cut slits in the top to allow steam to escape.) Decoratively crimp edges. In a small bowl, whisk together egg and 1 tablespoon of water. Brush top of pie with egg wash. Bake for 10 minutes, then lower heat to 350 degrees for 30 minutes more, or until top is golden and fruit is bubbly. Cool before slicing, and serve with hand-churned vanilla bean ice cream and a cup of coffee.

Chocolate Almond Pie

SERVES 6 TO 8

16 to 20 large marshmallows
Four 1½-ounce Hershey chocolate
  bars with almonds
½ cup milk

1 cup heavy cream
1 teaspoon vanilla
One 8-inch graham cracker crust

Melt marshmallows and candy bars in milk in double boiler. Remove from heat and cool. Whip cream until stiff and fold into cooled mixture. Add vanilla. Pour into prepared crust and chill. Good as is or top with whipped cream.

Strawberry and Cream Pie

SERVES 6 TO 8

1½ cups sliced and sweetened
  strawberries, drained

1 cup whipped cream

Cream together butter and powdered sugar; add eggs. Beat ingredients until fluffy. Spread over crust. Chill. Add topping.

TOPPING

8 tablespoons (1 stick) butter
1½ cups powdered sugar

2 eggs, beaten
One 8-inch graham cracker crust

Fold strawberries into whipped cream. Spread over chilled pie. Chill for at least 8 hours. Garnish with whole berries and mint leaves.

Thanksgiving Pie

SERVES 6 TO 8

3 eggs
1 cup dark corn syrup
½ cup sugar
4 tablespoons (½ stick) butter,
    melted

1 cup canned pumpkin
1 teaspoon vanilla
1 cup chopped pecans
One 9-inch unbaked pie shell
Whipped cream

Preheat oven to 350 degrees. With hand beater, beat eggs well. Beat in corn syrup, sugar, butter, pumpkin, and vanilla until well blended. Arrange pecans in bottom of pie shell. Slowly pour egg mixture over them. Bake for 1 hour or until knife inserted 1 inch from edge comes out clean. Serve with whipped cream.

Mama's Chess Pie

SERVES 6 TO 8

8 tablespoons (1 stick) butter
2 cups sifted cake flour

¼ teaspoon salt
3 to 6 tablespoons ice water

Cut butter into dry ingredients. Slowly add ice water. Knead dough and roll out on dough board, or press into bottom and sides of a 9-inch pie plate.

FILLING

½ pound (2 sticks) butter
2 cups sugar
7 egg yolks, beaten

1½ teaspoons vanilla
½ cup heavy cream
2 tablespoons cornmeal

Preheat oven to 350 degrees. Cream butter and sugar; add egg yolks, vanilla, and cream. Gently blend in cornmeal. Pour into chess pie pastry. Bake until light brown on top, about 35 to 45 minutes.

Lemon Meringue Pie

SERVES 6 TO 8

One 14-ounce can sweetened
   condensed milk
½ cup lemon juice
1 teaspoon grated lemon zest

3 egg yolks
One 8-inch prebaked pie shell or
   crumb crust

In medium bowl, combine milk, lemon juice, and zest; blend in egg yolks. Pour into cooled crust.

MERINGUE

3 egg whites
¼ teaspoon cream of tartar

¼ cup sugar

Preheat oven to 325 degrees. Beat egg whites with cream of tartar until soft peaks form. Gradually beat in sugar until stiff. Spread over filling; seal to edge of crust. Bake for 12 to 15 minutes or until meringue is golden brown.

Banana Cream Pie

SERVES 6 TO 8

⅓ cup plus ¼ cup sugar
3 tablespoons cornstarch
¼ teaspoon salt
1½ cups milk
2 egg yolks, lightly beaten

2 tablespoons butter
2 teaspoons vanilla
2 egg whites
2 bananas, sliced
One 9-inch prebaked pie shell

In a saucepan over medium heat, combine ⅓ cup sugar with the cornstarch and salt. Blend in milk, then egg yolks. Cook and stir until mixture thickens. Remove from heat; stir in butter and vanilla. Cool to room temperature. Beat egg whites until soft peaks form; gradually add ¼ cup sugar and beat until stiff peaks form. Fold into egg yolk mixture. In pie shell, alternate layers of banana slices and cream filling. Cover and chill. Top with whipped cream and additional sliced bananas, if desired.

Million-Dollar Pie

SERVES APPROXIMATELY 20

8 tablespoons (1 stick) butter
1 cup all-purpose flour
½ cup chopped pecans
One 8-ounce package cream cheese
1 cup powdered sugar

1 quart heavy cream, whipped with
 1 cup sugar until stiff
Two 3.4-ounce packages instant
 chocolate pudding mix
3 cups milk

Preheat oven to 350 degrees. In a 13 × 9 × 2-inch glass dish, melt butter and stir in flour and ¼ cup of the nuts. Bake about 20 minutes, until firm. Let cool.

First layer: Combine cream cheese, powdered sugar, and 1 cup of whipped cream. Layer over cooked nut crust.

Second layer: Combine instant pudding mix and milk. Layer over first layer.

Third layer: Combine remaining whipped cream and remaining chopped nuts. Layer over top. Keep refrigerated.   ❦ ❦ ❦ *The Lady & Sons*

Pastry for Two-Crust Pie

For extra-tender pastry, cut in half of the shortening until the mixture is like cornmeal; then cut in the remaining shortening until it is like small peas.

2 cups sifted all-purpose flour
1 teaspoon salt

⅔ cup Crisco shortening
5 to 7 tablespoons cold water

Sift together flour and salt; cut in shortening with pastry blender until pieces are the size of small peas. Sprinkle 1 tablespoon water over part of mixture. Gently toss with fork; push to side of bowl. Repeat until all is moistened. Form into 2 balls. Flatten each on lightly floured surface by pressing with edge of hand three times across in both directions. Roll from center to edge until ⅛ inch thick.

Chewy Pecan Cookies

YIELDS APPROXIMATELY 5 DOZEN

8 tablespoons (1 stick) butter
One 16-ounce box brown sugar
4 eggs, lightly beaten
½ teaspoon vanilla

2 cups all-purpose flour
1½ teaspoons baking powder
Pinch of salt
2 cups chopped pecans

Preheat oven to 300 degrees. Melt butter and sugar together in the top of a double boiler; remove from heat. Add eggs and vanilla. In a bowl, combine flour, baking powder, and salt. Add to egg mixture; mix well. Stir in nuts. Drop spoonfuls onto greased cookie sheet and bake for 15 to 20 minutes.   🍀 🍀 🍀 *The Lady & Sons*

Snickerdoodles

YIELDS APPROXIMATELY 4 DOZEN

1 cup Crisco shortening
1½ cups plus 2 tablespoons sugar
2 eggs
2¾ cups sifted all-purpose flour

2 teaspoons cream of tartar
1 teaspoon baking soda
½ teaspoon salt
2 teaspoons ground cinnamon

Preheat oven to 350 degrees. Cream shortening, 1½ cups sugar, and eggs. Sift together flour, cream of tartar, baking soda, and salt. Combine with egg mixture. Chill dough thoroughly and then roll into balls the size of a small walnut. Roll in mixture of 2 tablespoons sugar and the cinnamon. Bake for 8 to 10 minutes on an ungreased baking sheet until lightly browned but still soft.

Paula's Thin and Crispy Cookies

YIELDS APPROXIMATELY 3 DOZEN

2 cups all-purpose flour
½ teaspoon baking soda
1 teaspoon salt
2½ sticks butter, at room
    temperature
1 cup packed brown sugar
¾ cup sugar

1 egg
3 tablespoons water
1 tablespoon vanilla
1 cup milk chocolate chips
½ cup white chocolate chips
2 cups chopped pecans

Preheat oven to 350 degrees. Using a wire whisk, mix together flour, baking soda, and salt. Set aside. In a large electric mixing bowl, cream butter and sugars together. Add egg, water, and vanilla. Beat until combined. Slowly add flour mixture to creamed ingredients. Mix until combined. Stir in milk chocolate chips, white chocolate chips, and pecans. Using a regular-size ice cream scoop (holds approximately 2 to 2¼ ounces), place level scoops of batter onto a lightly greased cookie sheet, 9 scoops per sheet. Spray a piece of wax or parchment paper with nonstick cooking spray and lightly press down on each cookie. This makes thinner cookies. Bake for 12 to 15 minutes, or until desired color.

NOTE: I use more nuts than chips, because that's the way my family likes these cookies. Adjust the amount of goodies to suit your taste. I also mix the nuts, using pecans, walnuts, and macadamias.

Lady Lock Cookies

APPROXIMATELY 4 DOZEN

1 pound (4 sticks) butter
4 cups all-purpose flour
1 teaspoon salt

1 cup sour cream
1 cup buttermilk

Cut butter into dry ingredients. Add sour cream and buttermilk. Mix well. Divide into four parts, flour well, and fold like a rectangular envelope. Refrigerate overnight. Preheat oven to 375 degrees. Remove one part at a time, and roll thin. Make strips 1 inch wide and 7 inches long. Wrap around foil-covered clothespins. Bake for 15 minutes, or longer if needed. Set aside to cool.

FILLING

1½ cups Crisco shortening
8 tablespoons (1 stick) butter
1 cup sugar

1 egg white
2 teaspoons vanilla
½ cup hot milk

Cream together shortening and butter. Add sugar and beat well. Add egg white and vanilla; beat thoroughly. Add hot milk, 1 tablespoon at a time, and beat until creamy. Put into cookie press or pastry tube and fill cookies.

Butter Fingers

YIELDS APPROXIMATELY 100

1 cup chopped pecans
2½ cups all-purpose flour
¾ cup granulated sugar

½ pound (2 sticks) butter
1 teaspoon vanilla
One 16-ounce box powdered sugar

Preheat oven to 325 degrees. Combine all ingredients except for powdered sugar. Roll into small "fingers" or balls. Bake for 20 to 30 minutes. Roll immediately in powdered sugar.

Southern Tea Cakes

YIELDS 6 TO 8 DOZEN

This is a very old Southern recipe that has been handed down from one generation to another.

4 cups all-purpose flour	2 eggs
1 teaspoon baking soda	½ cup buttermilk
2 teaspoons baking powder	½ pound (2 sticks) butter, softened
2 cups sugar	1 teaspoon vanilla

Preheat oven to 350 degrees. In a large bowl sift flour, baking soda, and baking powder together. Add remaining ingredients and blend well. Dough should be soft. Roll dough out onto a floured surface until approximately ¼ inch thick. Cut dough into desired shapes and bake on a slightly greased sheet for 10 to 12 minutes.

Sliced Nut Cookies

YIELDS APPROXIMATELY 8 DOZEN

1 cup granulated sugar	1 teaspoon baking powder
1 cup brown sugar	1 teaspoon salt
1½ cups Crisco shortening	1 teaspoon ground cinnamon
3 eggs, beaten	1 teaspoon ground nutmeg
4½ cups all-purpose flour	½ teaspoon ground cloves
1 teaspoon baking soda	1 cup ground pecans

Cream sugars and shortening; add eggs. Sift together flour, baking soda, baking powder, and salt; add to sugar mixture. Add cinnamon, nutmeg, cloves, and nuts. Roll into several small, oblong rolls. Chill until cold. Preheat oven to 375 degrees. Slice dough into thin cookies. Bake for 12 minutes.

Goodies

YIELDS APPROXIMATELY 20

½ pound (2 sticks) butter
2 cups packed brown sugar
1 cup light corn syrup
½ teaspoon salt
1 teaspoon vinegar

1 teaspoon vanilla
⅓ cup peanut butter
1½ cups uncooked rolled oats
½ cup chopped pecans

Melt butter in large saucepan. Stir in brown sugar, syrup, salt, and vinegar. Cook over high heat to firm ball stage. Remove from heat. Stir in remaining ingredients; pour into greased 8-inch square pan and chill. Cut into squares. Wrap each piece in wax paper.

Low Country Cookies

YIELDS 15 TO 20

One 16-ounce box graham crackers
12 tablespoons (1½ sticks) butter
1 cup sugar
1 egg

½ cup milk
1 cup chopped pecans
1 cup or 3½-ounce can shredded coconut

Line a 13 × 9-inch pan with whole graham crackers. Melt butter in saucepan and add sugar. Beat egg and milk together; add to butter mixture. Bring to a boil, stirring constantly. Remove from heat. Add nuts, coconut, and 1 cup graham cracker crumbs. Pour over crackers in pan. Cover with another layer of whole graham crackers. Prepare topping.

TOPPING

2 cups powdered sugar
1 teaspoon vanilla

4 tablespoons (½ stick) butter
3 tablespoons milk

Beat all ingredients together and spread over top layer of crackers. Chill. Cut into squares.

Thumb Print Cookies

YIELDS 5 DOZEN

¾ pound (3 sticks) butter, softened
1 cup sugar
2 egg yolks
3 ¾ cups all-purpose flour

¼ teaspoon salt
1 teaspoon vanilla
Any tart preserves (plum, for
    example)

Cream butter and sugar. Add egg yolks. Sift flour and salt; blend into butter mixture. Add vanilla. Chill dough thoroughly. Preheat oven to 350 degrees. Shape dough into 1-inch balls and place on an ungreased cookie sheet. Make indentation in center of each with thumb; fill with preserves (jelly or pecan halves will also work). Bake for 15 minutes or until lightly browned. Cool slightly; remove to rack to finish cooling. These keep well in a tightly closed container.

Butter Cookies

YIELDS 6 TO 7 DOZEN

1 cup sugar, plus more for dipping
¾ pound (3 sticks) butter
2 egg yolks

1 tablespoon vanilla
3 cups bread flour

Gradually cream 1 cup sugar into butter. Add egg yolks and vanilla. Mix well. Add flour, gradually. Decide whether you want to use the dough in a cookie press, roll it out and use cookie cutters, or slice cookies. Shape the dough accordingly. Refrigerate for 2 hours or until ready to bake. Preheat oven to 375 degrees. Form dough into cookies, using whatever method you chose, and place on an ungreased cookie sheet. Bake for 10 to 15 minutes. Do not let them get brown. Use spatula to remove and place on rack to cool. When cool, dip in remaining sugar.

Grandma's Iced Georgia Squares

YIELDS APPROXIMATELY 20

¼ cup sugar
8 tablespoons (1 stick) butter
1 egg
1 cup all-purpose flour

½ teaspoon baking soda
1 teaspoon cream of tartar
Pinch of salt

Preheat oven to 350 degrees. Cream together sugar, butter, and egg. Sift dry ingredients together; add to egg mixture. Pour into greased 13 × 9 × 2-inch baking pan. Bake for 10 to 12 minutes. Cool. Prepare icing.

ICING

1 cup powdered sugar
4 tablespoons (½ stick) butter

½ teaspoon vanilla
Small amount of milk

Combine sugar and butter; add vanilla. Add just enough milk for desired consistency. Pour onto cooled baked batter. Cut into squares.

Cream Cheese Brownies

YIELDS 15 TO 20

Use Lady Brownies recipe above. Pour half the batter into a greased pan. Layer with this cream cheese mixture, then top with remaining batter, swirling it with a knife.

8 tablespoons (1 stick) butter,
   softened
One 8-ounce package cream
   cheese, softened

½ cup sugar
2 eggs
1 tablespoon all-purpose flour
1 cup chopped walnuts or pecans

Cream together butter and cream cheese. Add remaining ingredients; blend well. Swirl into brownie batter with knife edge.

❧ ❧ ❧ **The Lady & Sons**

Fudgie Scotch Ring

YIELDS 36 SLICES

One 6-ounce package semisweet
chocolate chips
One 6-ounce package butterscotch
morsels
One 14-ounce can sweetened
condensed milk

1 cup coarsely chopped walnuts,
plus 1 cup walnut halves
½ teaspoon vanilla

In top of double boiler, melt chocolate and butterscotch together with milk. Stir occasionally until mixture begins to thicken. Remove from heat; add chopped walnuts and vanilla. Blend well. Chill for 1 hour until mixture thickens. Line bottom of a 9-inch pan with a 12-inch square of foil. Place ¾ cup walnut halves in bottom of pan, forming a 2-inch-wide flat ring. Spoon chocolate mixture in small mounds on top of walnuts to form a ring. Garnish with remaining walnut halves. Chill until firm enough to slice.

Lady Brownies

YIELDS 15 TO 20

2 cups sugar
1 cup vegetable oil
4 eggs
6 tablespoons cocoa

1 teaspoon vanilla
1½ cups self-rising flour
1 cup chopped walnuts or pecans

Preheat oven to 325 degrees. Blend together sugar, oil, eggs, cocoa, and vanilla. Add flour; mix. Add nuts; spread into greased 13 × 9-inch baking dish. Bake for 25 to 30 minutes.   ❦ ❦ ❦ *The Lady & Sons*

Peanut Butter Bars

YIELDS 15 TO 20

8 tablespoons (1 stick) butter
½ cup peanut butter
1½ cups sugar

2 eggs
1 teaspoon vanilla
1 cup self-rising flour

Preheat oven to 350 degrees. Grease and flour a 13 × 9 × 2-inch pan. Melt butter and peanut butter in bowl over hot water. Add remaining ingredients. Stir until blended. Pour into prepared pan and bake for 25 to 30 minutes. Cool and cut into squares.

Aunt Glennis's Blonde Brownies

YIELDS 15 TO 20

3 eggs
8 tablespoons (1 stick) butter
One 16-ounce box brown sugar
2 cups self-rising flour
1 tablespoon vanilla

2 cups chopped walnuts or pecans
1 cup or 3½-ounce can shredded
    coconut (optional)
One 6-ounce package semisweet
    chocolate chips

Preheat oven to 375 degrees. Beat eggs and butter together; add sugar. Gradually add flour; mix well. Stir in vanilla. Fold in nuts, coconut, and chocolate chips. Bake in greased and floured 13 × 9-inch sheet pan for 25 to 30 minutes. Cool and cut into squares.

❧ ❧ ❧ *The Lady & Sons*

Peanut Butter Buckeyes

YIELDS 6 TO 7 DOZEN

One 12-ounce jar crunchy peanut
    butter (1½ cups)
One 16-ounce box powdered sugar
½ pound (2 sticks) butter

One 12-ounce package semisweet
    chocolate chips
1 bar paraffin

Mix together peanut butter, sugar, and butter and form into small balls; chill. Over medium heat in the top of a double boiler, melt together the chocolate and paraffin. Using a toothpick, dip each ball into chocolate and cover about three-quarters of the ball, leaving a brown round eye. Place on wax paper to cool.

Pecan Clusters

YIELDS 12 DOZEN

One 7-ounce jar marshmallow fluff
1½ pounds chocolate kisses
5 cups sugar

One 12-ounce can evaporated milk
8 tablespoons (1 stick) butter
6 cups pecan halves

Place marshmallow fluff and kisses into a large bowl. Set aside. Combine sugar, milk, and butter in a saucepan. Bring to a boil and cook for 8 minutes. Pour over marshmallow and chocolate, stirring until well blended. Stir in pecans. Drop by teaspoonfuls onto wax paper.

Peanut Butter Balls

YIELDS 18 TO 24

1 cup peanut butter
1 cup honey
2 cups powdered milk

1½ cups crushed cornflakes,
1½ cups finely chopped nuts of
your choice, or 1 cup powdered
sugar

Mix peanut butter, honey, and milk together to form very thick mixture. Roll out in small balls about the size of a walnut. Then roll in crushed cornflakes, finely chopped nuts, or powdered sugar. Place on wax paper and refrigerate. Roll balls in 1 cup melted chocolate before coating, if desired.

Old-Time Chocolate Fudge

YIELDS 36 PIECES

3 cups sugar
4 heaping tablespoons cocoa
3 tablespoons light corn syrup
1 cup evaporated milk

6 tablespoons butter
1 cup chopped pecans
1½ teaspoons vanilla

Mix sugar and cocoa; add syrup and milk. Cook in saucepan over medium heat until a small drop forms a soft ball in cold water (234 to 240 degrees on a candy thermometer). Remove from heat. Add butter, pecans, and vanilla. Beat with mixer or by hand. Pour into a slightly buttered oblong glass dish and cut into squares. Work fast, as mixture thickens quickly.

Five-Minute Fudge

YIELDS APPROXIMATELY 16 TO 24 PIECES,
OR ABOUT 2½ POUNDS OF CANDY

1⅔ cups sugar
⅔ cup evaporated milk
1 tablespoon butter
½ teaspoon salt
One 6-ounce bag semisweet
   chocolate chips

16 large marshmallows
1 teaspoon vanilla
1 cup chopped pecans

Combine sugar, milk, butter, and salt in a saucepan. Bring to a boil and cook for 5 minutes, stirring constantly. Add chocolate chips and continue to heat until chocolate is melted. Remove from heat and stir in marshmallows, vanilla, and nuts; mix well. Pour into shallow 8-inch square pan to cool; cut into squares.

Baked Apples

YIELDS 6 APPLES

Baked apples are so very good and can be served along with baked ham or roasted turkey as part of the meal. They may also be served as a dessert with caramel sauce.

6 same-size Granny Smith apples	2 tablespoons butter
1 teaspoon ground cinnamon	1 cup apple juice
¼ teaspoon ground nutmeg	6 sprigs fresh mint
½ cup sugar	

Preheat oven to 325 degrees. Core apples, being sure not to puncture bottom of apples, so the juices will remain. Skin ½ inch around top of apples at the opening. Fill each cavity with a mixture of cinnamon, nutmeg, and sugar. Top each apple with a teaspoon of butter. Place apples in casserole dish and pour apple juice around them. Bake for approximately 1½ hours.

CARAMEL SAUCE

8 tablespoons (1 stick) butter	¼ cup evaporated milk
1 cup light brown sugar	½ teaspoon vanilla

Melt butter; add brown sugar and evaporated milk in saucepan over medium heat. Cook until bubbly, stirring constantly. Continue to cook for 2 to 3 minutes. Remove from heat. Add vanilla. Place apples in individual compote dishes and top each with an ample amount of caramel sauce and a sprig of mint. Serve immediately.

❧ ❧ ❧ *The Lady & Sons*

Strawberry Mold

SERVES 12

I serve this as a congealed salad at holiday meals.

Two 3-ounce packages strawberry
   Jell-O
1 cup boiling water
Two 10-ounce cartons frozen
   strawberries

1 cup chopped pecans
3 medium bananas, sliced
1 cup crushed pineapple, drained
1 cup sour cream

Dissolve Jell-O in boiling water. Add remaining ingredients except sour cream. Pour half of mixture in salad mold; let chill. Cover with layer of sour cream, then top with remaining half of mixture. Refrigerate; chill until firm.

Savannah "Tiramisu"

SERVES 12 TO 16

2 dozen macaroons, crumbled
½ cup bourbon or rum
½ pound (2 sticks) butter
1 cup sugar
6 eggs, separated
2 ounces unsweetened chocolate,
   melted

½ teaspoon vanilla
½ cup chopped pecans
1 dozen double ladyfingers
¾ cup heavy cream, whipped with
   3 tablespoons sugar until stiff

Soak crumbled macaroons with bourbon or rum. Cream butter with sugar. Beat in lightly beaten egg yolks; add melted chocolate, vanilla, nuts, and macaroons. Beat egg whites until stiff; fold into chocolate mixture. Grease a springform pan; line with separated ladyfingers. Alternate layers of chocolate mixture with remaining ladyfingers. Chill overnight. Remove from pan and decorate with whipped cream.

Crème Caramel

SERVES 8

1 cup sugar
5 eggs
¼ teaspoon salt

3 cups milk
1½ teaspoons vanilla

Preheat oven to 350 degrees. Butter eight 6-ounce custard cups. In a small skillet over medium heat, melt ½ cup sugar, stirring constantly until it is a light brown syrup. Pour syrup into buttered cups. Place cups in baking pan for easy handling. In large bowl with mixer at low speed, beat eggs, salt, and remaining ½ cup sugar until lemon-colored. Gradually beat in milk and vanilla. Once mixture has settled, with all air bubbles out, pour mixture into cups. Put hot water into baking pan to within 1 inch of top of cups. Bake 1 hour or until knife inserted in center comes out clean. Cool, loosen custard with knife; invert.

VARIATION: Sprinkle ground nutmeg on top of each custard before baking.

Rice Pudding

SERVES 8

1 cup short-grain white rice
3 cups boiling water
½ teaspoon salt
One 14-ounce can sweetened
  condensed milk

4 tablespoons (½ stick) butter
½ cup raisins
1 tablespoon vanilla

Measure rice, boiling water, and salt into top of double boiler. Cook over rapidly boiling water until rice is tender, about 40 minutes. Stir in condensed milk, butter, and raisins. Cook, stirring frequently, over boiling water until slightly thickened, about 20 minutes. Remove from heat and stir in vanilla. Serve warm or cold.

❦ ❦ ❦ *The Lady & Sons*

Banana Pudding

SERVES 8 TO 10

At the restaurant, I no longer prefer the meringue topping but instead like fresh whipped. Of course, the pudding must be very cold before you add the whipped cream. Otherwise, the warmth from the pudding will break down the ingredients of the whipped cream.

¾ cup sugar
3 tablespoons all-purpose flour
2 cups milk
3 egg yolks

1 teaspoon vanilla
4 tablespoons (½ stick) butter
3 medium bananas, sliced
Vanilla wafers

Mix together sugar and flour and slowly add milk. This should be cooked in the top of a double boiler, but you can cook it over low to medium heat, stirring constantly until it thickens—do not leave it unattended. Slightly beat egg yolks and temper with a small amount of the hot custard; stir well. Add egg mixture to custard pot and cook 2 more minutes. Remove from heat and add vanilla and butter. Let cool. In a 13 × 9-inch casserole dish, alternate pudding, bananas, and wafers, beginning with pudding and ending with pudding. Add topping, if desired.

MERINGUE TOPPING

3 egg whites
¼ teaspoon cream of tartar

6 tablespoons sugar
1 teaspoon vanilla

Preheat oven to 350 degrees. Beat egg whites with cream of tartar and sugar until stiff. Add vanilla. Spread over pudding mix; completely seal around edge. Bake until desired brownness on top.

❦ ❦ ❦ *The Lady & Sons*

Walnut Praline Brie with Fruit

SERVES 4 TO 6

1 pound red or green grapes
¼ cup dark brown sugar
4 teaspoons butter

2 teaspoons light corn syrup
2 ounces chopped walnuts
1 small wheel of Brie (8 ounces)

Wash and divide grapes into clusters. Make praline: Place sugar, butter, corn syrup, and 1 teaspoon water in a small saucepan. Simmer for 3 minutes. Stir in walnuts. Cut Brie into wedges; arrange on round serving tray. Spoon 1 teaspoon praline mixture over each wedge. Garnish with grapes.

Peach Cobbler

SERVES 8 TO 10

8 tablespoons (1 stick) butter
1 cup sugar
¾ cup self-rising flour

¾ cup milk
One 28-ounce can sliced peaches in
*   syrup, undrained (see Variation)*

Preheat oven to 350 degrees. Put butter in deep baking dish and place in oven to melt. Mix sugar and flour; add milk slowly to prevent lumping. Pour over melted butter. Do not stir. Spoon fruit on top, gently pouring in syrup. Still do not stir; batter will rise to top during baking. Bake for 30 to 45 minutes. Good with fresh whipped cream or vanilla ice cream.   ❧ ❧ ❧ **The Lady & Sons**

VARIATION: When available, fresh fruit is wonderful. You may use fresh blueberries, strawberries, blackberries, cherries, apples, peaches, or pears. Simply clean, peel, and core 2 cups of fruit and mix with 1 cup of sugar and 1 cup of water. In a saucepan, bring mixture to a boil and then simmer for about 10 minutes. Stir often, making sure sugar is completely dissolved. Substitute this for the canned peaches.

Cooking Tips from
The Lady

1. Unless specifically instructed to put your dish in a cold oven to begin baking, you should *always preheat* the oven to the temperature required.

2. Always beat eggs before adding sugar.

3. Combine dry ingredients together when baking.

4. Add flour and milk to egg mixture alternately, beginning with flour mixture and ending with flour mixture for a lighter cake, muffin, or biscuit.

5. To eliminate odor from collards being cooked, add one washed, unshelled pecan to the collards pot before turning the stove on.

6. To determine whether an egg is fresh or not, place the uncracked egg in a glass of water. If it sinks to the bottom, it's fresh. If it floats, throw it out!

7. To make fluffier scrambled eggs, beat in a small amount of water instead of milk.

8. If baking a double-crust pie, brush top layer lightly with milk for a shiny crust; for a sweet crust, sprinkle with granulated sugar or a mixture of sugar and cinnamon; for a glazed crust, brush lightly with beaten egg. If you place the pie on a hot cookie sheet in the oven during preheating, it will ensure that the bottom crust will bake through.

9. You can always substitute 1⅔ cups all-purpose flour for 2 cups cake flour.

10. No buttermilk? Add 1 teaspoon distilled white vinegar to 1 cup fresh milk; let sour for 5 minutes.

11. Remember, 1½ cups corn syrup equals 1 cup sugar dissolved in ½ cup water.

12. To remove excess grease from soups, drop a lettuce leaf in and watch it absorb the grease. Repeat until the desired amount is removed. Discard lettuce.

13. To keep unused egg yolks fresh for future use, place in bowl and cover with 2 tablespoons of oil. They will remain fresh for 4 to 5 days.

14. If you're out of tomato juice, simply mix ½ cup tomato sauce and ½ cup water to create 1 cup of tomato juice.

15. If you want to achieve a lighter texture in your baking, add a teaspoon of baking powder to any recipe calling for self-rising flour or self-rising cornmeal.

16. Out of sweetened condensed milk? Make your own: Mix 6 cups whole milk with 4½ cups sugar, 1 stick of butter, and 1 vanilla bean (or 1 tablespoon vanilla). Cook over medium heat, reducing liquid, for 1 hour. Stir occasionally. Cool. Yields 4½ cups. This can be stored covered in the refrigerator for several weeks. Cut recipe in half for immediate use.

17. Red potatoes or "new" potatoes are far superior for use in any potato recipe. For great convenience in preparing a variety of potato recipes, keep cooked red potatoes in refrigerator at all times. They can be used on the spur of the moment for potato salad, hash browns, or French fries. They will keep at least a week in the refrigerator if they are well drained.

18. In many of the recipes by The Lady, you will find we make reference to our House Seasoning. The recipe is: 1 cup salt, ¼ cup black pepper, and ¼ cup garlic powder. Mix well. Store in shaker near stove for convenience.

19. If you're watching your fat intake, you can try substituting low-fat cheese, mayonnaise, sour cream, etc.

20. Never throw away chicken stock; fresh vegetables, such as peas, butter beans, turnip greens, collards, and rutabagas, are wonderful cooked in it. Stock may also be frozen for later use in soups and sauces.

Index

Acknowledgments

It's hard to believe it has been over seventeen years since a New York City editor transformed a collection of local recipes into a national best-seller. After completing fourteen cookbooks, *The Lady & Sons Savannah Country Cookbook* is still the one I go to first, and I jumped at the opportunity to refresh it. Truth be told, Jamie, Bobby, and I could not wait to have a new photo on the cover! I've added more recipes to make sure y'all have new ones to try, and I hope you rediscover the many Southern classics inside. In spite of the changes, I wanted to stay true to the original edition. John Berendt's introduction is timeless, and I dare not mess with perfection. The tribute from my sons is a special part of the original edition—a lovely surprise added by Jamie and Bobby that I only discovered when I opened the printed book for the first time.

This book was created out of love and with the support from all of my family, friends, staff, and guests. My most heartfelt thanks goes out to each and every one of you, including Mildred C. Ambos, Pat Andres, Ernest Bartley, Trina Bearden, Amy Beaver, John Berendt, Diane Berryhill, Nancy Blood, Holly Brantley, Mike Carnahan, Jamie Chabot, Joshua Charpentier, Christina Cheves, Bob Christian, Todd Churco, Leroy Clayton, Becky Cohen, Theresa Lynn Creo, Roger Crews, Kevin Crumbley, Carolynn C. Cundiff, Janet Di-Claudio, Jessie Ruth Dixon, Amy Dupuy, Susan Dupuy, Judge Tom Edenfield, Frances Finney, Felicia Gaines, David Gaynor, Lorianne Greenlee, Jean Gregory, Maria Griffin, Anthony Groover, Ashley Groover, Ann Schuburger Hanson, Captain Judy Helmey, Corrie Waye Hiers, Don Hiers, Earl "Bubba" W. Hiers Jr., Elizabeth Hiers, Glennis Hiers, Jill R. Hiers, C. McCall Holmes, Cathy Holmes, David Howard, Dion Hurd, Rance Jackson, Ineata "Jellyroll" Jones, Jacklyn Miller, Sheila M. Mims, Jody Moyer, Karen Nangle, George A. Ort III,

Kelley P. Ort, Peggy P. Ort, Jacqueline R. Patton, Michael Peay, Shelly Peay, Erick Pineda, Paul Powell, Jeanne Powers, Daniel Reed, Michelle Groover Reed, Peggy Richardson, Virginia K. Robertson, Helen Rooks, Bill Schumann, Esther Shaver, Kristen Short, Clark Smith, Dorothy S. Smith, Steven P. Starling, Brendan Sweeney, Charlene Wagner, Suzette Dupuy Wagner, Denise Watson, Claire Watts, Chris White, Melvin Williams, Willie Wilson, and Mary Evelyn Young.

Twenty years ago, we worked hard to make The Lady & Sons restaurant a success, and as I reflect on those long days, I so appreciate everything in my life today. We recently opened a second restaurant, Paula Deen's Family Kitchen, in Pigeon Forge, Tennessee, and memories of creating the first came flooding back. Trusted staff members opened the new location, but I just couldn't help myself and taste tested the recipes to ensure they were truly honored. Once again, I enjoyed the excitement of busy hot days in the kitchen, working toward the opening of a new restaurant.

I thank all of my business partners for creating products that I am very proud of: the magazine *Cooking with Paula Deen*; my furniture line, made by Universal Furniture; my cookware and bakeware, created by Meyer Corporation; my food products; and the new Hugs pet food line. I have been blessed, and I am forever grateful.

This lady and her sons have all found love, and there is more than enough to go around. My Captain Michael Groover brings joy and laughter to my days. I have watched Jamie and Bobby mature from wonderful boys into loving husbands, and I love my daughters-in-law, Brooke and Claudia. I am now a grandmother, and my five grandbabies, Jack, Matthew, Henry, John, and Sullivan, keep me young. I look forward to the future with excitement and gratitude.